Report

Growing Good:
Growth, Social Action and Discipleship
in the Church of England

Hannah Rich

Foreword by Stephen Cottrell,
Archbishop of York

The Final Report of the GRA:CE Project

"...for the growing good of the world is partly dependent on unhistoric acts; and that things are not so ill with you and me as they might have been, is half owing to the number who lived faithfully a hidden life, and rest in unvisited tombs."

George Eliot, Middlemarch

Foreword

The Faith in the City report in 1985 led to a re-imagining of the Church of England's mission and role in society, a legacy carried on by the Church Urban Fund it established. While criticised at the time as overly political, the report was as much about calling the church to learn afresh what it meant to love our neighbours as it was about the duties of government.

The task of imagining what the Church of England should do – of asking how it should serve as the national church – is one that is never quite complete. As the context evolves, so must our Church. It is not a case of blending seamlessly into whatever backdrop is provided by the political or economic forces of the day. Rather, it is about understanding how the themes and rhythms of the Kingdom of God are at once both resonant and dissonant with the time and place we find ourselves.

If the early 1980s felt like a moment at which we needed deep and prayerful reflection on the Church of England's ministry, how much more now!

When Theos and Church Urban Fund embarked on this project three years ago, they could hardly have imagined the tumult into which this report would be launched. The unprecedented challenges of the COVID-19 pandemic prompted a re-evaluation of many aspects of everyday life and have plunged the whole world into economic instability. In addition, our country is about to begin a new chapter outside the formal structures of the European Union, and the union of the United Kingdom looks increasingly more fragile.

The church too, finds itself at a turning point, having quickly had to embrace new online and hybrid forms of worship alongside pastorally ministering to local communities and continuing vital social action work throughout this difficult year.

The future shape of both the country and the Church is yet to be defined. Like many other institutions, the Church of England will have to evolve. I firmly believe this evolution lies in a more simple and humble church whilst remaining Christ-centred and Jesus shaped. I long for us as Christian sisters and brothers to be a Church vibrantly fulfilling its mission to form disciples who are compelled to love their neighbours. This will evidence itself in a variety of ways, from small and unsophisticated acts of kindness to the large-scale charitable projects in which many of our church communities are engaged. As Christians, we can't help but show our love in this way because God, our Heavenly Father first loved us.

In a fractured society, where people increasingly only relate to those within their own tribes, social action creates meaningful relationships spanning divisions of race, faith, social class, and political ideology. Participation in it, as this report emphasises, has the potential to genuinely transform both individuals and communities. These are all small 'signs of the Kingdom' and I believe we should strive for more, as we bring the healing balm of the Gospel to our nation, for this is our vocation.

I warmly welcome the publication of this report, and it is my hope and prayer that it can make a defining contribution to the Church in the coming decades.

Stephen Cottrell

Archbishop of York

Contents

Contents

Acknowledgements	8
Executive summary	11
Introduction	16
1. Definitions	26
2. The context	40
3. What helps churches grow? Qualitative insights	56
4. What helps churches grow? Statistical insights	131
5. Conclusion and recommendations	143
Appendix 1: Qualitative sampling	157
Appendix 2: Defining church size	158
Appendix 3: Quantitative survey sample	164
Appendix 4: Survey questions	166

Acknowledgements

I would like to express a particular thank you to:

— My Theos colleagues, in particular Paul Bickley, Elizabeth Oldfield, Madeleine Pennington, Nick Spencer and Lizzie Harvey.

— Church Urban Fund staff especially Jessamin Birdsall, Heather Buckingham and Amy Page.

— Theos research assistants Katherine Ajibade, Simeon Burke, Hannah Eves, Laura Moulton and Mehr Panjwani for research support at various stages of the project.

— Bev Botting, Louise McFerran, Charlotte Sibtain and the Church of England Research and Statistics team for support with the quantitative work and providing data.

— The project advisory group for their constant encouragement, challenge and guidance, with a particular mention to Liz Graveling for her 100% attendance record.

— Andy Delmege and Mark Betson for lending us their events to host round tables.

— Ellen Loudon, Simon Fisher and the congregations of St Helens, Widnes and Warrington deaneries for their participation in the quantitative survey.

— All the clergy and congregations who kindly gave their time during the qualitative research, and to all those who shared their stories in interviews and conversations over a cup of tea. A special thanks to those whose generosity extended as far as offering the hospitality of vicarage spare bedrooms and kitchen tables.

— Clare Kendall for the photography and Hazel Southam for additional reporting of the stories.

— Polly Parrott and the publishing team at the Bible Society for their tireless work in designing and producing this report.

— Sir Halley Stewart Trust and Hartham Church Charitable Trust, without whom the research would not have been possible.

— My parents, Colin and Hilary Rich, who provided many, many cups of coffee throughout the writing of this report during the lockdown period.

Advisory group

The following people contributed to the advisory group at some point in the three years:

— Paul Bickley, Research Fellow, Theos.
— Jessamin Birdsall, Head of Research and Evaluation, Church Urban Fund.
— Dr Bev Botting, Head of Research and Statistics, Church of England.
— Dr Heather Buckingham, formerly Director of Research and Policy, Church Urban Fund.
— Dr David Clifford, University of Southampton.
— Patrick Coldstream, former Trustee, Church Urban Fund.
— Dr Andrew Davies, Reader in the Public Understanding of Religion and Head of the Department of Theology & Religion, University of Birmingham.
— Revd. Canon Andy Delmege, Canon Missioner at Birmingham Cathedral and formerly Executive Director, National Estate Churches Network.
— Dr Sarah Dunlop, Tutor in Practical Theology, Ridley Hall, Cambridge.
— Philip Fletcher, Trustee, Church Urban Fund.
— Revd. Dr David Goodhew, Vicar, St Barnabas Church, Middlesbrough, England and visiting Fellow of St John's College, Durham.
— Dr Liz Graveling, Research Officer, Church of England.
— Canon Paul Hackwood, formerly CEO, Church Urban Fund.
— Revd. Dr. Stephen Hance, National Lead for Evangelism and Witness for the Church of England.
— Revd. Simon Harvey, Vicar, St Mary's with St Peter's Church, Bury St Edmunds.
— Revd. Dr Anderson Jeremiah, Trustee, Church Urban Fund.
— Ven. Andy Jolley, Archdeacon of Bradford.
— Dr Rachel Jordan-Wolf, formerly National Lead for Evangelism and Witness, Church of England.
— Revd. Ivor Lewis, Curate, St John's & St Peter's Ladywood, Birmingham.
— Revd. Canon Dr Ellen Loudon, Director of Social Justice and Canon Chancellor, Diocese of Liverpool.
— Jon Miles, formerly Director of Development, Church Urban Fund.
— Dr Madeleine Pennington, Head of Research, Theos
— Christina Rees, Trustee, Church Urban Fund.
— Hannah Rich, Senior Researcher, Theos.
— Revd. Chris Russell, Archbishop of Canterbury's Adviser for Evangelism and Witness.
— Ben Ryan, formerly Head of Research, Theos.
— Nick Spencer, Senior Fellow, Theos.
— Selina Stone, St Mellitus College.
— Rachel Whittington, CEO, Church Urban Fund.

Executive summary

Over the past decade, the contribution that the Church of England makes to society through its social action has increased, reflecting an increase in the demand and expectation for it. At the same time, church attendance in the country has continued to decline; by most key metrics, attendance at Church of England services fell by between 15% and 20% from 2009-2019. This is the paradox facing the Church of England in 2020: the national church of a nation which is increasingly reliant on its social action and yet less and less spiritually connected to it.

The culmination of three years of extensive qualitative and quantitative research, including over 350 interviews in over 60 parish communities across England and new analysis of existing parish data, this report explores the relationship between social action, church growth, and discipleship in the Church of England. It finds that social action can be a route to church growth in both numerical and spiritual terms. It is one of the key ways in which congregations can build wider networks of relationships which can result in people initiating a faith journey and joining the church.

We do not suggest that that there is a single, infallible way to grow a church. We do however identify a set of characteristics shared amongst churches that are growing numerically, and flourishing through their engagement in social action, and helping people grow in their faith.

— We find that the church grows in number and depth when it is **present** in and connected to its local area, which may be manifested through its social action. Churches which are visible, or are recognised as being active in giving to their community, are more likely to grow. The congregational culture as well as the physical presence of the church can both help and hinder growth in this way, for example in the way they can create the perception of a church as open to its community or the reverse.

— The Church of England's longevity and **perseverance** in presence can make it well placed for this. Congregation growth often occurs after years of focused activity or engagement in meeting the needs of a community.

— **Hospitality** and **generosity** are significant for church growth. Social action which is perceived as 'instrumental' or paternalistic often fails to engage people in the wider community. Hospitality and generosity communicate genuine willingness to engage with and invest in the community as it is. Congregations that grow through their social action are also likely to be adaptable and embracing of life's complexities. Church leaders and congregations demonstrating **adaptability** in discipleship and worship is therefore critical to cultivating these meaningful relationships.

— **Participation** in social action can also offer a practical route into faith for people who weren't previously part of the church community and might not have considered exploring faith before. Volunteering in church-based projects or activities enables people to reappraise churches and their beliefs, and often leads to people re-engaging with Christian faith.

Crucially, social action leads to church growth when it enables congregations to develop meaningful relationships with those they would not otherwise have done, or who might not otherwise have come into sustained contact with the church. These relationships are a key mechanism through which the church grows and also through which individuals grow in their own personal faith, but are not always linear or straightforward.

Drawing on the identified characteristics of flourishing churches, this report recommends:

— That the Church of England explore new ways of measuring church growth and impact. Existing measures do not adequately capture the contextual and local factors or the changing shape of church life. Just as in 2020, due to the COVID-19 pandemic, congregational worship has changed shape and the measurement of it is seeking to adapt to this, there are important aspects of church life that have not previously been captured.

— Further, that congregations and church leaders should be equipped to think about social action, discipleship and church growth in an integrated way rather than as three independent concepts, particularly through the training of ordained and lay leadership as well as the preaching of the church. This could include the development of a new 'How to Make a Difference' course to integrate discipleship with volunteering.

— That while churches can often focus on invitation in terms of social events or discipleship programmes, they should equally see their social action projects as primary sites of invitation and be expectant of the relationships that can grow through it.

— That a Church of England volunteering service for people of all faiths and none should be established. This would connect people of goodwill to local projects, channelling the untapped reserves of goodwill witnessed during the pandemic and opening up opportunities for

new relationships between the church and the wider
community.

Introduction

Emma is a young mum who comes to church for the first time as a last resort, knowing only that it hosts the food bank to which she's been referred. She is pleasantly surprised to be greeted by friendly faces. Someone hands her a mug of tea and a plate of toast, and offers to hold her baby while she eats and someone else prepares her parcel of groceries. They chat to her and suggest she might like to come to the church's toddler group, or bring her older children along to the Messy Church congregation that meets on Saturday afternoon for fun activities, worship and a meal. To Emma, the church extends the offer of community, not just commodities.

Having recently been widowed, Stanley is invited by his next-door neighbour to come to a lunch club for the over 65s held by the local church. Over a hot meal of beef casserole followed by sponge pudding and custard, he finds himself enjoying conversation with the guests, many of whom tell him that they attend the church. He hasn't been to church himself since his wedding day fifty years ago, but finds the way they talk about the service intriguing and decides to go along on Sunday. For Stanley, his new friendships pave the way for a newfound relationship with God.

Candice has recently moved to a new neighbourhood and is keen to find a way to contribute to her local community. She hears that the church at the end of her road hosts a night shelter for homeless people during the winter months, so she emails the vicar to ask if she can help out. The church is delighted at her offer of support, and she begins volunteering to cook for the night shelter guests once a fortnight. Having never considered it before, she starts to explore Christianity and joins a group at the church for people interested in faith. Eventually, Candice's participation in the wider life of the church offers her the opportunity not only to effect change, but to be changed herself.

These stories highlight the value of the local church, in ways that are familiar to many. The work of food banks, lunch clubs and night shelters, among other forms of social action, is largely an accepted part of our national life and the fact that the church is at the heart of providing them is no longer exceptional. Yet, at the same time, there is a growing sense of existential crisis about the Church of England as the national church and an apparent decline in attendance at odds with its enduring practical and relational contribution to local communities.

The seminal *Faith in the City* report in 1985, which led to the establishment of the Church Urban Fund (CUF), set as part of its aim "to reflect on the challenge which God may be making to Church and Nation".[1] It explored the role of the church in inner city areas and housing estates, and stimulated a wider conversation about the social and economic role of the church in national life. Three decades on, many of the questions it addressed remain pertinent. While the external pressures of the economy and the changing sociocultural role of the Church of England to the nation are significant, the church is not without its own internal challenges.

It might be that these twin crises and their solutions are also intertwined. Stories like those of Emma, Stanley and Candice are heard anecdotally in local church communities across the country and hint at the possibility that social action might be linked to both numerical church growth and the development of individuals' Christian faith. To those engaged in church social action in communities across the country, this connection may seem familiar, even intuitive. But is there anything more to it than an intuition?

This research project has sought to investigate this relationship between church growth, social action and discipleship, exploring the hypothesis of a positive correlation through robust research grounded in the lived experience of Anglican congregations across England.

The Church Growth Research Programme (CGRP), which concluded in 2014, made a significant contribution to understanding of factors that contribute to the growth of the church, looking specifically at the Church of England. Like this research, it drew on both qualitative and quantitative evidence in developing robust proof for what seemed anecdotally true to those working in local ministry, reflected in the title of its summary report *From Anecdote to Evidence*.[2] While it engaged clearly and helpfully with the theme of church growth, and is thus cited where relevant here, it left unanswered questions of how social action and discipleship might be integral to growth, on which the GRA:CE Project has tried to build.

The CGRP report acknowledged that,

> *There is no single recipe for growth; there are no simple solutions to decline. The road to growth depends on the context, and what works in one place may not work in another.*[3]

This research finds likewise. While there is no single way in which social action and discipleship interact to contribute to growth, this report has identified several key factors that are observed when this does occur and which facilitate growth through social action. In identifying these, it provides valuable insight for anyone seeking to understand how our established church is changing and what that means for its future growth and flourishing.

Having defined the research terms in Chapter 1, the report sets out the context of the church and the perceived decline that gives rise to the imperative for congregational growth, considering this against wider socioeconomic challenges and growing reliance on church social action (Chapter 2).

Chapter 3 then outlines from in-depth qualitative research the common characteristics of churches that are growing and flourishing through the integration of social action and discipleship. In Chapter 4, the report draws on analysis of existing and new quantitative data to outline factors which influence church growth and present a congregational picture of social action and its effects.

Chapter 5 gives recommendations for church institutions, church leaders and local congregations based on these findings, suggesting how these core characteristics can be developed in the life of the church and thus lead to spiritual and numerical growth.

a. Research methodology

The research used a mixed-methods approach, combining qualitative and quantitative analysis in order to understand both the stories and statistics at the heart of church growth, social action and discipleship. The first phase was qualitative and the second quantitative.

Qualitative

The qualitative phase began with a series of 17 preliminary interviews in March-May 2018 with individuals including staff of the national church institutions, diocesan stakeholders, principals of Anglican theological colleges, social action practitioners, academics and bishops. These focused on different understandings of the three research elements in turn (social action, discipleship and church growth) and their possible connections. We asked each preliminary interviewee to define each element in turn and then discuss how they would conceive of or hypothesise the relationship between them. Insights from these interviews were used in shaping the discussion guide and questions used in the full qualitative research process.

The second part of the qualitative research was a series of parish-level case studies over an eighteen-month period from June 2018-December 2019. We visited 66 case study parishes and conducted semi-structured interviews with 337 individuals, encompassing over a hundred churches and at least one parish in every diocese of England. The parishes were chosen using a purposive sampling strategy to represent the full breadth and diversity of the Church of England in terms of church size, congregation demographic, geography and church tradition. (A full explanation of the sampling strategy and a breakdown of the sample can be found in Appendix 1.)

The case study parishes were all recruited by the lead researcher, who also carried out the majority of the interviews with some support from Theos research assistants. In all but one case study, the clergy was the initial point of contact in approving participation and arranging interviews and visits.

Participants included clergy, church staff, lay leaders, congregation members, volunteers, guests of church social action and other community stakeholders such as local head teachers.

Written consent was sought from participants at the beginning of each interview prior to the audio recording. They were told that, while interviews would be transcribed and quotes might be used verbatim in this report, they would not be identifiable and could thus speak openly.

Interviews were conducted at a time and place convenient to each participant. Locations chosen included church halls, food bank storage cupboards, coffee shops, community cafes, lunch clubs, quiet corners of toddler groups, post-service coffee and, on one occasion, over lunch in a local pub.

In 47 of the 66 parishes, researchers also conducted observations of church-based social action, discipleship groups and/or midweek church services and engaged in informal conversations with those involved. These were not recorded or transcribed, but researchers kept field notes.

Interview transcripts and field notes were coded and analysed by the lead researcher using NVivo software. A framework of over a hundred key codes was developed iteratively.

Two roundtables were also held as part of the qualitative research. One was hosted in collaboration with the National Estate Church Network and attended by 15 practitioners and clergy working in estate ministry. The second roundtable was held at a national gathering of c.40 rural mission officers from the Church of England and Methodist Church. The round-tables sought to explore the specific nature of the relationship between church growth, social action and discipleship in the estate and rural parish context respectively, and their particular contextual challenges and opportunities. These were recorded and summary notes were written.

Quantitative

The second phase of the GRA:CE research was quantitative, beginning with additional analysis of the existing *Statistics for Mission* data as outlined in Chapter 4. We analysed the data gathered by the Church of England's Research and Statistics team annually, in terms of the demographic and geographic characteristics of the parishes, to explore whether there are any common trends among growing churches. As explained in Appendix 2, as part of this we also considered in some depth the perception of church size and what might constitute large, medium and small congregations in the Church of England, which shaped the sampling of parishes for the qualitative work.

The original plan was for a nationwide congregational survey to be conducted using the Big Church Survey platform in conjunction with the Church of England, which would have interrogated the research questions within a wider sample. This was planned to take place in spring 2020 in order to allow analysis of the completed qualitative phase to shape the questions.

The survey was intended to ask questions about people's involvement in social action, and whether they felt this had changed or affected their faith and their relationship with their community.

Unfortunately, due to the COVID-19 pandemic and lockdown period that meant congregations were not meeting in person, the Big Church Survey was postponed. We therefore worked with the Church of England's Research and Statistics team to develop a smaller survey. An additional question was added asking how social action had shifted because of the crisis.

With the support of Liverpool diocese, we were able to implement this in three deaneries in the diocese in June 2020 and received 130 responses from 22 parishes. Whilst we are grateful to the clergy and congregations who contributed to this under challenging circumstances, it is unavoidably a much smaller sample that we had originally intended to achieve in the quantitative phase.

Nonetheless, we include in chapter 4 some analysis of this data, along with indications of what it might mean for the national church. Full details of the quantitative survey sample can be found in Appendix 3 and the survey questions are reproduced in full in Appendix 4.

1 Archbishop of Canterbury's Commission on Urban Priority Areas, *Faith in the City - A Call for Action by Church and Nation* (London: Church House Publishing, 1985).

2 Church Growth Research Programme, *From Anecdote to Evidence: Findings from the Church Growth Research Programme 2011-2013* (London: Church of England, 2014), available at www.churchofengland.org/sites/default/files/2019-06/from_anecdote_to_evidence_-_the_report.pdf

3 David Voas quoted on p7 of *From Anecdote to Evidence.*

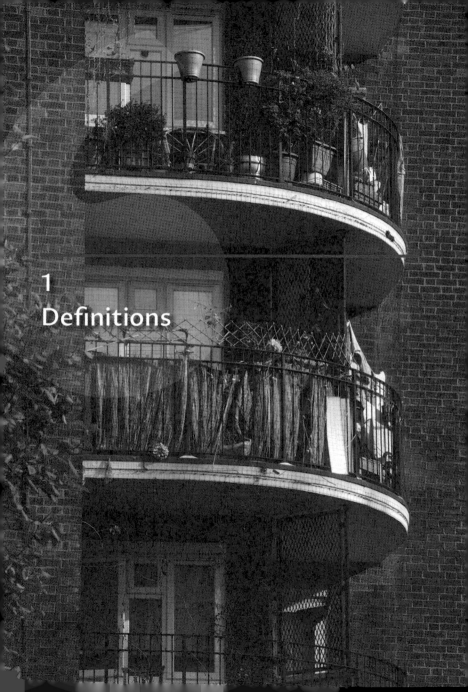

1
Definitions

While this report focuses on the connection between the three elements – church growth, social action and discipleship – it is important to define what it meant by each of the research terms in turn. Throughout the qualitative research, the definitions were kept deliberately broad in order that as wide a range of parishes and individuals as possible felt able to participate. The insights and perspectives of research participants have therefore informed the definitions given here.

a. Defining church growth

Church growth may be understood as an increase in the number of people actively affiliating to and attending a congregation or church community. Wider, deeper, stronger, larger and younger are some of the adjectives most commonly used to describe the *sort* of growth churches seek in size, faith, influence and demographic diversity. They are also key concerns for the Church of England, given the decline in attendance, ageing congregations and questions around the sustainability of its ministry in places. However, for our purposes, the spiritual dimensions of growth come under the concept of discipleship, as defined later on here.

Numerical measurements of growth are necessary in order to be able to state with some degree of confidence whether or not the church is growing, both nationally and locally. The practical theologian and Bishop of Penrith Emma Ineson argues that while numbers are not the be-all and end-all of ministry, there are both biblical and pragmatic reasons why counting is important. She notes that the Old Testament is full of examples of counting, with justice and accuracy seeming to matter. However, she goes on to say that, "counting is a provisional, earthly need necessary to govern and fill and subdue the earth while we have other fallible human kings and rulers."[1]

There are some within the Church of England who are ambivalent about the concern for numerical growth in the Church of England; a number of interviewees in the qualitative research felt the need to emphasise unprompted that they are "not opposed to the growth agenda but..." However, it is the language or approach to numerical growth and its measurement that some feel uncomfortable with, not that they think it is actively a bad thing to want to see the church grow.

Former Bishop of Chelmsford Stephen Cottrell – now Archbishop of York – highlighted some of the tensions surrounding the discussion and measurement of growth:

> Instead of talking about bums on seats, let's instead talk about disciples being made and hearts changed; or best of all, let's talk about lives transformed. It seems to me that the best way of answering the question, what sort of growth do we need, is not to say shall it be numbers or shall it be impact, or even to say shall it be both, as if these things were different from each other, but to say let it be growth in transformation.[2]

This underlines how church growth is not independent from discipleship, either conceptually or practically. Nor is it completely separate from the transformative impact of social action on individuals and community. **Bringing these three together might offer a richer understanding of growth, rooted in local church experience as well as quantitative rigour,** which leads us to the 'what' and 'how' of growth measurement.

In terms of numerical growth, it is important not only that it is measured, but also what is measured and how it is done. The Church of England defines and measures church growth in terms of parish-level trends over a ten-year period. A particular parish is considered to be 'growing' if the congregation has experienced statistically significant numerical growth in the last decade and vice versa for decline. This is measured by either the average weekly attendance or usual Sunday attendance for each parish. At least half of all parishes are described as inconclusive, i.e. have not demonstrated a conclusive pattern of growth or decline over ten years, but this covers a multitude of nuances and scenarios. For example, if a congregation has lost a significant number of members, whether due to death or population transience, but maintained its size, it has effectively grown whilst staying the same. Conversely, the description of a parish as growing or declining does not control for contextual factors that may have an influence on growth, such as birth and death rates, migration flows or changes in the population of the parish as a geographical area.

This illustrates the distinction between the reality of church growth and the quantitative measurement of it. The experience of what church growth 'feels like' can sometimes be at odds with the quantitative classifications. Whilst 10% of congregations are classed as growing according to the statistics, a greater proportion of parish communities describe experiencing some form of growth qualitatively speaking, even if this is difficult to express or capture quantitatively.

Examined in connection with social action and discipleship, growth in the dispersed church as well as the gathered church is critical. Anglican theologian Stephen Spencer suggests that considering only the increase or decrease in size of the gathered church "distort[s] the nature of the church," arguing that growth in dispersal should also be factored in.[3] Paying attention to the dispersed church and nurturing its growth is of heightened importance in the current context of adapting church life in response to the COVID-19 pandemic.

The qualitative phase of this project is especially important in allowing us to identify the context-specific ways in which congregations recognise they are growing, and where the statistical definition of church is mismatched with the empirical experience of a growing church.

In this report, we therefore define church growth as primarily numerical, but in broader terms than attendance. Where relevant, we also identify the other ways in which particular case study churches are observed to be growing and ultimately suggest ways in which the measurement of church growth might develop to reflect the reality of the contemporary church better.

b. Defining discipleship

Throughout this research, discipleship has been the most contested and hardest to define of the three elements, by both clergy and laity alike. This confirms David Goodhew's finding that "there remains significant confusion and inaction with regard to Christian initiation and promotion of discipleship, which needs to be overcome" in order to achieve growth.[4] The CGRP noted that growth is linked to "intentionally nurturing disciples"[5] and the second of the core Five Marks of Mission – "to teach, baptise and nurture new believers" – reflects this.

The concept of discipleship originates from the New Testament accounts of Jesus' first followers and more specifically the twelve individuals called to be his closest disciples.

In the New Testament, the word is rooted in learning and a teacher-apprentice dynamic between Jesus and his disciples. The evangelists, writing in Greek, drew on the relationship that Ancient Greek philosophers had with their students or *mathētés*, who learned through observing and modelling a way of life not just learning a set of intellectual principles. This has clear parallels in the Jewish tradition Jesus was familiar with, in terms of the relationship between a rabbi and his *talmidim*, the teacher and his students. In Hebrew scripture, the *talmidim* were those who had literally left everything behind to follow a rabbi and learn from him a way of life as well as knowledge and religious tradition. **To be a Christian disciple is therefore to identify as a follower of Jesus and seek to model his character in all of life, not just to adhere intellectually to Christianity as a set of beliefs.**

Despite its prevalence in the New Testament, discipleship has not always been a central concept in church history across traditions, nor is it universally employed. Historically, the notion of catechesis was a more widespread way of expressing how people join and are formed in Christian community. Discipleship has become a more common concept in speaking about these processes, shifting from something cognitive and didactic to something more practical and exploratory. This is perhaps in response to a wider culture in which inherited Christianity is waning and prior intellectual or cultural knowledge cannot be taken for granted.

As with the language of church growth, there are some within the Church of England who are not comfortable with the language of discipleship, although it remains the dominant paradigm of Christian formation in the contemporary church. Some have expressed concern that that the focus on discipleship above all other aspects of church life represents the 'evangelicalisation' of the Church of England. Sociologist of religion Linda Woodhead, for example, criticised what she sees as the "theologically peripheral concept of 'discipleship'," suggesting that it led to a hierarchical distinction between leadership and followership, clergy and laity.[6]

There is also a perception that the idea of discipleship belongs primarily to a particular type of church and accompanying demographic associations of the term. For example, in our qualitative research, we heard from clergy in smaller and/or rural churches that it is not a word they felt their congregations would relate to naturally, as it is seen as primarily something that larger and/or urban churches do, suggesting it is perceived as a resource-heavy and organised activity. As with growth, however, it seems it is the language and approach that some object to, rather than the idea itself.

Discipleship is not a linear process; as one individual told us, it is not "a straight line from atheist to archbishop". As we shall go on to explore in this report, embracing life's complexity is an important aspect of church life, and this means recognising that discipleship can also refer to the journey towards faith that people may be on long before they acknowledge themselves as a Christian. It is articulated broadly as an ongoing, whole-life process of becoming more like Jesus, which does not necessarily begin with a faith commitment. Even when it occurs organically, through practical participation in the life of the church, discipleship ultimately involves a recognition of who Jesus is. It might begin without full understanding of this, but it is paramount that it emerges along the way.

As with social action, there is a tendency observed in many churches to view discipleship as something programmatic or initiative-focussed. When asked about their church's notions of discipleship, many participants responded by outlining the formal courses or programmes run by the church to help its members grow in faith. The guidelines for applications to the Church of England's Strategic Development Fund (SDF) include numbers attending worship, numbers joining discipleship groups, numbers involved in volunteering/leadership roles, giving figures and numbers of baptisms or confirmations as possible indicators of increasing discipleship. Together, these can present a picture of the spiritual depth of church growth and discipleship, not only the numerical scale of it.

At its simplest, a disciple is someone who seeks to follow Jesus and become more like him. **We therefore understand discipleship as an ongoing process by which people grow in Christian learning and practice through following Jesus and becoming more like him.** Considered in relationship to social action, this practical element is particularly important.

c. Defining social action

Social action has been defined as "people coming together to help improve their lives and solve the problems that are important in their communities", and is seen to comprise a spectrum from formal volunteering schemes through to informal, relational forms of social action.[8]

Christian social action can be seen as distinct from its civic equivalents in some ways. First, while much church social action looks like distinct interventions on particular social issues, much is an expression and extension of the relational life of a church community, resulting in informal but important structures of care. Therefore, church social action occupies a spectrum ranging from project to presence. Throughout the research, it was emphasised to participants that social

action on all points of the spectrum was relevant to the study. A breadth of activity is therefore reflected in the parishes included in the qualitative research, along with the breadth of issues the church is tackling through its social action, from food poverty to loneliness, from homelessness to asylum seeker support.

Second, there are differences in character and motivation. It is a way of making Christian beliefs manifest in social life, both within and beyond the boundaries of the church community. In a previous Theos report, Nick Spencer suggested that we might refer to "Christian social liturgy" in order to express the combination of the two greatest commandments – loving God and loving neighbour simultaneously – without losing the sense of balance between the two.[9]

Social action is sometimes interpreted as solely being about projects like food banks or toddler groups, which are the archetypal examples. Throughout the research, it was emphasised to participants that social action in the form of organised projects is not the only relevant example. There was a correlation observed in our qualitative research between the sorts of churches most likely to view discipleship in terms of programmes and those likely to see social action through a similar bureaucratic distinction. Smaller parishes and those in rural areas were both more likely not to describe their work as social action and the same category were equally likely not to see discipleship as something relevant to them. It is therefore important to define social action such that it encompasses what Williams et al call the "differently constructed local cultures of charity" in urban and rural communities.[10]

A previous Theos/CUF report described congregational social action as **relational, incarnational and spiritual**.[11]

It is relational in that it is oriented towards the building of communities and rich interpersonal relationships, not towards the provision of services. It is incarnational in that it emphasises being part of a community, rather than the dynamic of client/provider relationships, and the integrated approach is often highlighted as what differentiates it from statutory services such as job centres. (A report from Church Urban Fund in 2012 found that relationally focused projects that "treat people with intrinsic worth" are most effective at breaking down barriers between churches, community stakeholders and service users.[12]) It is spiritual in that it is galvanised by collective and individual religious commitment, although this not always articulated by a clear "theology, a narrative or an overall ethos behind that action".[13]

Congregational social action therefore is the collective activity of congregations to establish means of support or effect social change in ways consistent with Christian social witness.

It is also worth noting that the contribution made by the Church of England through occasional offices (in particular funerals), civic services and faith schools, whilst beyond the scope of what was explored in this research, are also considered by some as part of the church's social action. These can enable the church to build relationships with people with whom they are not already in contact, in a way we observe is important if social action is to lead to growth and discipleship.

The breadth of theological traditions within the Church of England means that there is considerable diversity in how churches think about social action. However, the stereotype that evangelical churches focus on discipleship and growth, and social action was the preserve of more liberal or Catholic churches no longer holds. We have seen churches of all traditions who focus on social outreach in their parishes and are both growing and flourishing, and seeing that as a means to discipleship.

1 Emma Ineson, *Ambition* (London: SPCK Publishing, 2019), p. 65.

2 Stephen Cottrell in Beth Green, Angus Ritchie, Tim Thorlby, *Church Growth in East London: A Grassroots View* (London: Centre for Theology and Community, 2016), p. 38.

3 Stephen Spencer, *Growing and Flourishing: The Ecology of Church Growth* (London: SCM Press, 2019), p. 51.

4 David Goodhew with Ben Kautzer and Joe Moffatt, *Amalgamations, Team Ministries and the Growth of the Church* (Durham: Durham University Research Report, 2013).

5 Church Growth Research Programme, *From Anecdote to Evidence...*,

6 Linda Woodhead, 'The challenges that the new C of E reports duck', *Church Times*, 23 January 2015, available at: www. churchtimes.co.uk/articles/2015/23-january/comment/opinion/ the-challenges-that-the-new-c-of-e-reports-duck

7 Church of England, 'Strategic Development Funding guidance and resources', available at: www.churchofengland.org/about/renewal-reform/funding-mission-and-growth/strategic-development-funding/ strategic-development

8 Cabinet Office, *Social action: harnessing the potential - discussion paper* (2015), available from: www.gov.uk/government/publications/ social-action-harnessing-the-potential.

9 Nick Spencer, *Doing Good: A Future for Christianity in the 21st Century* (London: Theos, 2016).

10 Andrew Williams, Paul Cloke, Jon May and Mark Goodwin, 'Contested space: The contradictory political dynamics of food banking in the UK' in *Environment and Planning* 48:11 (2016), p. 2296.

11 Paul Bickley, *Good Neighbours: How Churches Help Communities Flourish* (London: Church Urban Fund and Theos, 2014).

12 Church Urban Fund, *Growing Church through Social Action: A study of actively-engaged and growing churches* (2012), available online at: www.cuf.org.uk/sites/ default/files/PDFs/Research/Quantitative_report_FINAL2.pdf https://cuf.org. uk/uploads/resources/Growing-Church-through-social-action-quantitative-new_2012.pdf

13 Samuel Wells with Russell Rook and David Barclay, *For Good: The Church and the Future of Welfare* (Norwich: Canterbury Press, 2017), p. xxii.

2
The context

ENTRANCE

a. Disaffiliation and decline in attendance in the Church of England

The significance of our three core themes – church growth, social action and discipleship – lay in the fact that they are at the centre of the Church of England's mission and self-understanding. They are priorities at a local and national level.

The Five Marks of Mission, which are shared across the whole Anglican Communion, are:

> To proclaim the Good News of the Kingdom; to teach, baptise and nurture new believers; to respond to human need by loving service; to seek to transform unjust structures of society; to challenge violence of every kind and to pursue peace and reconciliation; and to strive to safeguard the integrity of creation and sustain and renew the life of the earth.

In 2010, the Church of England committed to "serving the common good as a national church" as one of its quinquennial goals, representing the priorities of the church's General Synod for the coming five-year period. The imperative for growth in Church of England congregations in order to achieve this was enshrined in the second of the 2010 goals, which referred to a commitment to facilitate the growth of the Church in numbers and depth of discipleship. The third quinquennial goal from 2010 was about reimagining the Church's ministry in the new decade. This has arguably gained heightened importance a decade on, as adapting worship and ministry in response to the COVID-19 pandemic has required a large degree of imagination and creativity.

The Archbishops' Council subsequently drew on these goals throughout the objectives it set for 2017-2020.[1] At the time of writing, these objectives are reaching their conclusion and the upcoming meeting of Synod will likely reformulate

these for the coming five years, but will no doubt continue to pursue similar priorities for the Church.

There is a building tension within these objectives. The need for much of what the Church of England offers through its service of the common good is growing, yet at the same time, the number of people who worship in and affiliate with the Church of England has and is continuing to decline. The church finds itself battling for legitimacy as a national institution and losing traction within the national sense of identity, both culturally and spiritually. It is also experiencing a diminished capacity to address social need.

Ten years since the quinquennial goals first set numerical growth as a priority, the data show little evidence that decline has been reversed in any significant way and thus the need for growth remains.

The most recent *Statistics for Mission* release, consisting of data from 2019, observed a continual gradual decline in attendance at Church of England services, according to all key measures of weekly attendance. By most key metrics, attendance fell by between 15% and 20% from 2009-2019.[2] In 2019, the usual Sunday attendance was 690,000 and the average weekly attendance was 854,000 – that is, between 1.5% and 2% of the national population.

The Church of England is not just seeing falling attendance figures, but also a marked downward trend in affiliation. According to the *British Social Attitudes Survey* (BSA), Christian affiliation fell from 66% to 38% between 1983 and 2018.[3] Among Christian denominations, Anglicanism accounts for the sharpest decline in affiliation, with those identifying as belonging to the Church of England or its sister churches in Scotland and Wales falling from 40% in 1983, to 22% in 2008, to just 12% in 2018. This appears starkest when the data are broken down by age group; whilst a third of respondents over the age of 75 described themselves as Anglican, only 1% of 18-24-year-olds did.

To take London as an example, a recent Theos report found that it is the youngest and most religious place in the country, but also the least Anglican, which suggests that the crisis facing the Church of England is more complex than a generational shift away from religion.[4] In an increasingly pluralist society, where religion is no longer a given, "even vaguely religious people who in the past would have identified themselves as belonging to the Church of England or another group no longer do so."[5] Any residual cultural affiliation to the Church of England appears to be in freefall and is likely to accelerate.

However, as scholars like David Goodhew argue, the dominant story of decline in the Church of England is in fact more nuanced.[6] At a granular level, usual Sunday attendance is seen to have increased in 10% of parishes and decreased in 41% of parishes, while 49% of parishes displayed no conclusive trend over the past decade.[7] The overall result of these trends remains a church in which more individual parishes are declining than growing, and this has been the case for a number of years. There are, however, clear pockets of growth[8] and, as the Church Growth Research Programme demonstrated, plenty of examples of Anglican churches growing.[9]

Furthermore, there may be ways in which the primary metrics for understanding congregation growth or decline do not reflect the changing shape of the church, or indeed the different ways in which people could be engaging in Christian community. At present, growth trends are considered primarily in terms of Sunday attendance, but Sunday does not hold the societal value it once did. Rhythms of work and leisure have shifted. There is therefore scope for our understanding of what it means to belong to a church to be extended beyond Sunday attendance.

The "Worshipping Community" measure of congregation size, introduced in 2012, aimed to contribute to this, giving an indication of how many people go to church regularly or identify as part of the church community.[10] It encompasses many of those who encounter the church first through its social action, then through its worship rather than the reverse. This is seen to have declined by 3% in the last five years[11], although remains largely stable over a longer period and has not yet been collected for the ten-year period over which growth can be reliably measured. In the recommendations section in the final chapter of this report, we discuss further the possibility of alternative metrics that might better reflect the reality of the church today.

b. The Church of England's evolving social role

At the outset of this research in late 2017, the material and social conditions of the country seemed especially urgent. The result of the 2016 European Union referendum result had revealed latent political and social divides and, in many cases, deepened them. The 2017 general election had resulted in a minority government, with the political instability that entailed. Further, this came after a decade of austerity and the retrenchment of state provision at a national and local level left a gap that the community sector has sought to fill, with mixed success. At a local level, churches of all kinds have been reshaping themselves for this challenging landscape.

mitre
International
Goddess
Victory
97005 USA
sport
crafted
life.

17-year-old Immanuel joined the football club at St John's Church in Hoxton on a Saturday when he was 13. He is now on a youth ministry work experience scheme at the church, and hopes to be an engineer.

"I saw a notice about football at St John's on a Saturday. I thought it was a good opportunity. The people were friendly. We did a warm up and we split into teams and have competitive games.

"People around me have had the experience of wanting to go to a football court and people from that postcode won't recognise them. This community is a lot more friendly and accepts everyone.

"I love how football brings people together. We still play with people from church, but there are refugees who come here. They don't speak English. But we speak with our feet, and it's fine. I've definitely made a lot of friends.

"During football one of the youth workers approached me and said it would be good if I joined the youth work with children. We have table tennis and Playstations. It's a fun experience. It's quite energetic. They come here and run around, but it's fine. The ability to adapt to their needs is exciting.

"I couldn't have seen myself doing this, but I am doing it. I don't think the opportunity would have come up for me. Others are on their Playstations all day or hanging out with themselves, probably not using their time for the best possible way.

"I'm taking an engineering course and I want to do that. But if God calls me to the youth ministry, I would not mind."

Research by CUF and Theos in 2014 found that 10 million people in England would say that they or their family has accessed community-based services provided by the church (not including acts of worship) in the last year.[12] The 2019 *Statistics for Mission* data indicated that 77% of Anglican churches were involved in one or more forms of social action, representing involvement in a total of 35,000 individual projects.[13] Most recently, a report from the National Churches Trust found that church buildings create £12.4 billion in economic value every year, of which £10 billion is the 'non-market value' of social and mental wellbeing contributed.[14]

The Common Good objective set by the Archbishops' Council in 2017 of "transforming our society and communities more closely to reflect the Kingdom of God through loving acts of neighbourliness and service to all" drew on what the church had long been engaged with in a myriad of ways at a local level. However, this is now often understood within the prism of cuts, either local or national, creating or exposing new needs. A church community worker we interviewed in summer 2018 described the economic and relational effects of public spending cuts on their parish:

One of the things we identified about two years ago was that because of all the cutbacks, there was a growing sense of isolation in our community. In our ward, 49% of children live in poverty. We have a high level of unemployment and lots of issues around debt. But we picked up from listening to people that they were feeling more and more alone because of austerity and cuts in services.

While the focus of this research has not been to count how much social action the Church of England engages in, or even to measure its economic value, almost two years of fieldwork in parishes across the country leaves one in little doubt that the need is real and not going away.

To take one example, Church Urban Fund data in 2017 showed that 93% of Church of England churches were involved in some way in the provision of food banks. A third of congregations said they provided volunteers and 69% provided supplies or financial support.[15]

It is worth noting at this point that all the stories in this report were gathered before the pandemic crisis was even on the horizon. (The qualitative phase began in early 2018 and the final interview took place in late 2019.) The socioeconomic consequences of the pandemic will only deepen the challenges faced by these communities and increase the importance of the social action recounted.

It is nigh impossible to think of a social action project, be it food banks, debt advice centres, job clubs or homelessness shelters, which will not now be in greater demand.

The Trussell Trust reported that food bank use in April 2020 was up 89% on the same month in 2019 and the number of food parcels given to children increased by 107%, figures which had already increased significantly year-on-year since 2015.[16] Research by the Church of England and Child Poverty Action Group research among low-income families found that 82% of respondents stated that the pandemic had affected their ability to meet the cost of food specifically.[17]

The pandemic has also brought the issue of holiday hunger to the fore – the problem of food poverty when children are unable to access school meals – which affects around three million children in the UK.[18] This was highlighted publically by footballer Marcus Rashford's campaign to ensure that children in receipt of Free School Meals were provided for during the summer holidays in addition to the extended period of school closures due to lockdown. However, churches have long recognised holiday hunger as a problem in their communities; 52% of Church of England churches are involved in supporting holiday clubs that address this and 30% run one themselves.[19]

It should be noted that this growth in social action is not planned – a tactical attempt to soften the Church of England's image. Rather, it has come in response to economic and political contingencies. This means the social action of churches is often a factor of congregations just trying to deal with what is in front of them. A key example of this is how a number of churches in our study were having to shape and reshape their work around growing populations of refugees and asylum seekers due to Home Office resettlement areas within their parish.

> *They come to us and it's like a litmus test of who is being abused in our world. If they stopped sending asylum seekers here, the whole ministry would stop.*

In many places, those joining the community in this way have been a source of significant growth and blessing to the local church. Growth in the Persian migrant contingent in Church of England congregations was such that in 2019, a Farsi language translation of the liturgy was launched.[20] This has also led to the development of what one church leader described as "an accidental network" of churches working with asylum seekers. In some cases, clergy are involved in asylum tribunals for their congregants, which are time consuming and not necessarily within their prior expertise.

As one vicar admitted:

I joke that before I was ordained, I didn't know what an asylum seeker was. I didn't know where Iran was. Now I advise the Home Office on Christian conversion for Iranians.

Reactive social action of this type is a challenge to congregations which are not necessarily well disposed to it. It cannot be assumed, for example, that the clergy and congregations in resettlement areas would actively have chosen to work with asylum seekers as part of their ministry. Churches are not charitable initiatives consisting only of people who have actively sought opportunities to help those in need, but also worshipping communities and places where people make a journey of faith. Social action might be seen as integral to discipleship, but this is not always the case.

Unsympathetic or apathetic attitudes to the poor exist within congregations, just as in wider society, and attending church does not appear to change people's underlying attitudes to poverty and inequality significantly or inevitably. A Church Urban Fund report in 2012 showed that churchgoers then were less sympathetic to those in need that in the 1980s when the *Faith in City* report was published.[21] As we will go on to explore, this suggests that the connection between discipleship and social action might be made more explicit.

Over the last decade, the retreat of the state has led to the Church fulfilling its welfare and community-building capacity, incentivised by the Big Society ideology propounded in the early years of the coalition government. At the time, Rowan Williams, then Archbishop of Canterbury, drew on the work of the nineteenth century theologian John Neville Figgis in highlighting how the idea of "a community of communities" encouraged by the Big Society was intrinsically Anglican.[22]

If the Big Society sought to empower local communities and encourage civic involvement, partnership and volunteering, the Church of England and its parish system was surely well placed to enact this.

As Sam Wells acknowledges however, "the danger is that, for all their growing social impact, churches become more defined by what they believe about the state's role than what they believe about their own."[23] The way in which food banks have become embedded in the national social infrastructure is a prime example of this, in a manner some consider problematic. Part of the complexity is that "food banks sit at the cross-road of religious, political and economic forces".[24] The numbers of food parcels facilitated by congregations is objectively good but the society in which they are necessary can still be challenged.

As a nation, we worship and affiliate to the Church of England in ever lower numbers, yet we remain deeply connected to it through its contribution of social action.

It is paramount that the Church of England is confident in its spiritual and practical identity as a national religious institution as it seeks to mediate the same relationships of state v church social action once again. The intersection of civil society, the church and the role of the state is as live a topic as ever, faced with the likelihood that the coming decade will be shaped by a global financial crisis at least as significant as the last. Williams ended his appraisal of the Big Society by suggesting it might be a watershed moment for the country and "that if voluntary bodies, churches, other religious communities are willing to join in that argument and pursue it vigorously, we may yet be in for a couple of rather interesting decades in the politics of this country." For better or for worse, this has certainly proved to be the case and the church must prepare itself for what it will mean to be the national church in an era of economic insecurity, post-Brexit and post-pandemic.

During the COVID-19 pandemic, various media commentators and reports accused the Church of England of having disappeared from public life. At a local level, this was far from the case, with local churches stepping up their social action to meet increased demand. More broadly than the current COVID-19 crisis, the value of local churches and what they offer to the community is clear, but this does not appear to translate into positive institutional recognition.

1 Archbishops' Council Objectives 2017-2020, available online at: www. churchofengland.org/sites/default/files/2019-09/AC%20Objectives%202017- 2020.pdf

2 Church of England Research and Statistics, Statistics for Mission 2019 (London: Church of England Research and Statistics, 2020), available online at: www. churchofengland.org/sites/default/files/2020-10/2019StatisticsForMission. pdf.

3 John Curtice, Elizabeth Clery, Jane Perry, Miranda Phillips and Nilufer Rahim (eds.), British Social Attitudes: The 36th Report (London: The National Centre for Social Research, 2019), available online at: www.bsa.natcen.ac.uk/ media/39293/1_bsa36_religion.pdf

4 Paul Bickley and Nathan Mladin, Religious London: Faith in a global city (London: Theos, 2020).

5 John Curtice et al., British Social Attitudes... p. 7.

6 David Goodhew, 'Church growth in Britain, 1980 to the present day' in David Goodhew (ed.), Church growth in Britain, 1980 to the present (Abingdon: Routledge, 2012), p. 3-20.

7 Church of England Research and Statistics, Statistics for Mission....

8 Peter Brierley, Capital Growth: What the 2012 London Church Census Reveals (Tonbridge: ADBC Publishers, 2014).

9 Church Growth Research Programme, From Anecdote to Evidence...

10 The Worshipping Community metric of congregation size was introduced in 2012 and aims to capture a wider picture of the congregation size, based on churches' recording of the people who attend church regularly (e.g. once a month or more) or would do so if not prevented by illness or temporary absence. This represents a broader understanding of who is counted in the church community than either the usual Sunday or average weekly attendance, which were previously used.

11 Church of England Research and Statistics, Statistics for Mission...

12 Paul Bickley, Good Neighbours: How Churches Help Communities Flourish (London: Church Urban Fund and Theos, 2014), p. 10.

13 Church of England Research and Statistics, Statistics for Mission...

14 National Churches Trust, The House of Good (London: National Churches Trust, 2020).

15 Church Urban Fund, Church in Action 2017....

16 Trussell Trust, Lockdown, lifelines and the long haul ahead: The impact of Covid-19 on food banks in the Trussell Trust network (Salisbury: The Trussell

Trust, 2020), available online at: www.trusselltrust.org/wp-content/uploads/sites/2/2020/09/the-impact-of-covid-19-on-food-banks-report.pdf

17 Child Poverty Action Group and Church of England, Poverty in the Pandemic: The impact of coronavirus on low-income families and children (London: CPAG and Church of England, 2020), available online at: cpag.org.uk/policy-and-campaigns/report/poverty-pandemic-impact-coronavirus-low-income-families-and-children

18 All Party Parliamentary Group on Holiday Hunger, Hungry Holidays: a report on hunger amongst children during school holidays, (London: APPG on Holiday Hunger, 2017).

19 Church Urban Fund, Church in Action...

20 Izzy Lyons, 'Church of England to hold first service in Farsi after huge rise in Iranian converts' in The Telegraph, 3 March 2019, available online at: www.telegraph.co.uk/news/2019/03/03/church-england-hold-first-service-farsi-huge-rise-converts/

21 Church Urban Fund, Bias To The Poor? Christian Attitudes To Poverty In This Country, (Church Urban Fund and Christian Action on Poverty, 2012), available online at: cuf.org.uk/resources/bias-to-the-poor-a-study-of-christian-attitudes-to-poverty-in-this-country

22 'How should churches respond to the Big Society?' – speech given by Archbishop Rowan Williams, 23 July 2010, full transcript available online at: aoc2013.brix.fatbeehive.com/articles.php/571/how-should-churches-respond-to-the-big-society-rowan-williams

23 Samuel Wells with Russell Rook and David Barclay, For Good: The Church....

24 Charles Roding Pemberton, Bread of Life in Broken Britain: Food Banks, Faith & Neoliberalism (London: SCM Press, 2020), p. 3.

3

What helps churches grow? Qualitative insights

As mentioned in the introduction, previous research has found that there is no single, infallible way to grow a church. However, from our analysis of the qualitative research, we find that there are several key factors that characterise churches that are growing or flourishing through social action.

These factors pertain to the culture and environment of the church, not only the practical situation. However, the characteristics described here are specific to churches whose growth in number and discipleship is demonstrably connected to their engagement in social action.

We do not suggest that the type of social action is what contributes to church growth (i.e. the research does not indicate that churches running food banks are more likely to grow than churches running coffee mornings, for example). Rather, we find that **the manner in which social action is approached is what makes it conducive to congregational growth**, or not.

In short, the characteristics of a flourishing church are those which promote meaningful relationships: **social action leads to church growth where it enables churches to grow meaningful relationships with people they would not otherwise have done, or who might not otherwise have come into sustained contact with the church community**, and these relationships are the mechanism through which churches grow. So too, congregations thrive and grow in discipleship when they are equipped and prepared to embrace the complexity of life and circumstances represented by those who meet the church through social action. Participation in social action can offer a valuable and significant route into faith and discipleship for people who weren't previously part of the church community.

These characteristics were drawn from coding and analysis of the qualitative interviews. We observe these to be common characteristics of those churches within the sample that are growing by at least one congregational metric. Insights from churches that are either declining or inconclusive have also shaped and strengthened our understanding of these ideas, and it is explicitly stated where this is the case. Furthermore, there are numerous examples where participants described their church as 'growing' and went on to discuss the importance of one or more of these concepts, but where the attendance is not statistically classed as growing. Again, we state where this is the case along with an explanation of why this might be i.e. whether church growth is a misperception here, or whether that church might be growing in ways that are harder to measure.

a. Presence

The church grows in number and depth when it is present in and connected to its local community, which may be manifested through its social action.

One of the defining aspects of the Church of England is its presence in every community, facilitated by how the parish system recognises pastoral and spiritual responsibility for the entire country and its population at a local scale. Every community and every individual has a local parish church, regardless of whether they attend. Collectively, this is the footprint that both constitutes and justifies the church's national presence even in an era where its perceived value as a national institution is diminishing. In fact, where there is residual fondness for the Church of England, this is often expressed with reference to its local rather than national incarnation.

One vicar expressed this as a fundamental part of the church's ministry:

> *There is a ministry of presence that we have and that we're called to have. So what does victory look like for the Church of England? I think victory sometimes looks like staying.*

The visible presence that the church has in a community is key to the growth of the congregation and the effectiveness of its social action at a local level. **It is important not only that the church is doing good, but also that it is known for the good it does**, and growth in presence is therefore sometimes framed as a precursor to growth.

A strategic awareness of what the presence of the church looks like to its community is important. We encountered parishes where the church building is in the heart of the community geographically and this renders its presence in community life natural.

In one of these, where the building is prominent in a busy market square, the church's core social action was the presence of congregation members in the church building every day of the week to welcome passers-by in for conversation, refreshments and prayer. The congregation has almost doubled in five years since this became an intentional part of church life, including a number of people returning to church after a long absence. The clergy here also report a notable increase in the number of occasional offices (baptisms, weddings and funerals).

The recently arrived curate felt that:

> *It's a church at the heart of its community, both sort of physically and spiritually. Physically, it's got a great position*

*right at the heart of the marketplace and I think that everything
we do tries to put the church at the heart of the community.*

This is not, however, an approach that all churches have
recourse to; we visited other communities where the parish
church is harder to find physically, such that the natural
footfall of local residents past the building is lower. An
awareness of what the presence of the church's ministry might
mean in a specific parish context is critical for growth, perhaps
more so than any particular characteristic of that ministry.
Even between parishes we might categorise as similar, there
is not one universal picture of what presence looks like. In
several rural case studies, for example, the church was the
central institution and main community building in the
village. In another not dissimilar rural case study, however, the
congregation described the need for the church to rediscover
its own distinctive presence in a thriving village with over 50
other community groups.

In one inner-city parish where the church building was
positioned in the midst of densely-populated terraced streets,
we heard about a congregation who held a regular coffee
morning called 'Open Church', described as a time during
which the church would be open for the community to come
for conversation and refreshments. However, the doors of the
church building remained closed throughout and there was
little physical indication outside of what was going on inside.
A local resident walking past, for example, would not have
known they were welcome to come in. The intention behind
the activity (and its name) was hindered by the invisibility of
the church's presence.

This continued until a new member of the community
remarked on this apparent disconnect. The deliberate decision

was made to open both of the double doors at the entrance to the church; something we were told had typically only happened previously in order to facilitate funerals. This represented a small change in culture and practice, which was described by congregation members as having been significant for the impact of the church in its wider community.

A helpful lens through which to consider this is Cameron et al.'s 'Four Voices of Theology' model, which distinguishes four aspects of theology in practice: normative, formal, espoused and operant. The last two in particular are important here. The espoused form of theology is "embedded within *a group's articulation of its beliefs*" whereas the operant theology is "embedded within the *actual practices of the group*".[1] According to this model, the same community or congregation may have multiple theological voices that can sometimes contradict or contrast with each other. In the case study above, the espoused theology of the 'Open Church' was at odds with the operant theology expressed by the closed doors. An authentic theological voice is important for church growth; congregations should therefore consider how their culture and social action helps or hinders the coherence of it, as in this example.

In a number of case study parishes, the narrative of growth began from a point where the local community did not realise the church was still open. In one suburban parish, an individual who had recently joined the church community with no prior faith background spoke about how they had previously had the false notion that the church was closed:

> I'd always lived locally and I had tried several times in my life to get into this church over a number of years and every time I'd come, it had been closed. I thought it was a closed church,

actually, from looking at the outside of it. I'd never seen anybody go in or out.

For this individual and others we heard from in various places, the fact that the church building "looked closed" gave the impression that the church community was itself no longer present. In one church where attendance was declining, but whose leadership were keen to reverse this, a member of the Parochial Church Council (PCC) described the challenge of "trying to rebuild the understanding that there is an active church in the community here."

The vicar of one church highlighted how, when they arrived in the parish, they were struck by how many people in the local community thought the church was closed:

The number of people that said that they thought the church had closed down years early was really shocking. The whole outside space of the church was totally overgrown with brambles and weeds. The whole site looked like it was closed down.

In this example, the congregation was already engaged in a substantial amount of social action, much of it hosted in the building, but this was unbeknown to those outside the church.

In one parish, we saw how growth had begun with changing the outer appearance of the building so that the community was aware it was there. This was a collective effort, with members of the congregation and local residents involved in the work of clearing the churchyard and painting. The immediate impact of this was that the social action activities already hosted and supported by the church saw an increase in drop-in visitors, as did the Sunday service, which has doubled in size and now includes a number of individuals who were previously guests of the church's social action.

A lay leader illustrated the impact of the changing building on the church's social action:

People just turn up for help. They can see that life is here now and they wander in and want to look round. You can see that life is here now. That's the difference.

Elsewhere, in a city centre parish, the dismantling of a literal barrier wall that had surrounded the vast church building had been a fundamental and symbolic part of developing the church's mission, which ultimately led to significant numerical growth. Together with intentional connection with local residents, what had been an enclosed church building became a thriving presence within a busy square. The church rediscovered its ancient role at the physical heart of the community and the congregation grew.

The reverse can also be true; one member of clergy spoke about arriving in a parish to discover how, in its finances, the congregation prioritised the repair of a perimeter fence over social action or charitable giving. This was, the vicar felt, inadvertently indicative of a cultural and theological outlook in which the congregation presented itself as "a gated community of wonderful praying Christians".

The importance of a congregational culture characterised by its openness, tied to the visible openness of the building, was a recurring theme in growing church communities.

The physical presence of the church can also point to the reason for its action and worship. German theological Dietrich Bonhoeffer wrote that, "the space of the church is the place where witness is given to the foundation of all reality in Jesus Christ" and in this sense, we observe that the church building can be central to connecting social action with discipleship and growth.

As one church staff member put it:

The great thing about here is the church as a building really speaks about the love of God. I don't know if you felt it when you came in. Sometimes people just cry when they walk into the building.

In numerous places, we encountered social action taking place in the church building itself, either by necessity or by choice. Several churches did not have church halls or additional spaces and therefore host everything in the same space as worship. This can be used to symbolise the faith motivation behind the action. For example, one church ran a second-hand school uniform swap and used the altar rail to display the clothes. Volunteers expressed that this was a way of gently enabling visitors to interact with every aspect of church life, whether or not they were familiar with the church as a place of worship or only as the place they brought their children for a new uniform.

This importance of the church as somewhere sacred is what distinguishes it from secular charitable organisations. This is critical if social action is to lead to the discipleship of those involved.

In one small town parish, we heard the story of a woman who came regularly to a church coffee morning but asked if a cross on the wall could be removed from the space where it met because she was uncomfortable with it. Whilst they refused, this was a wake-up call for volunteers here that in their eagerness to welcome the whole community, they had not differentiated themselves enough from any other civic institution, to the point where those visiting did not recognise the spiritual value of the place. Their social action work was thriving, but it was not growing the congregation.

This is a prime example of how the culture and intention around social action, and not merely the action itself, is instrumental in growth. The same form of social action – for example the coffee morning – can enable discipleship in one place and not in another, if the culture is different.

Particularly in rural communities, we heard how the presence of the church is still known, accepted and valued. Knowing the church and feeling a part of it is seen as a unique part of community life in the rural context, even where this does not necessarily translate into large attendances every Sunday. In rural parishes, particularly those with smaller congregations scattered across a team ministry with a large geographical area, the presence of the church need not necessarily mean that every building is open, all of the time. This might not always be feasible.

In one case study, we encountered an Ecumenical Missional Partnership spanning a mixture of Anglican and Methodist congregations in a number of small villages across a vast geographical area. Keeping the buildings open where possible sent a message to each village that it is valued by the church. The politics of village identity meant that it mattered not only that there was a church locally, but that there is a church present in that village. It was a form of witness; a way of stating, like Jacob at Bethel in Genesis 28, that "the Lord is in this place".

The partnership between villages as well as denominations allowed for social action to be shared between communities that could not have sustained it alone; for example, a holiday club for local children run by volunteers from numerous churches which intentionally moved between villages in order to be present locally to all those involved at least once. Across the dozen Anglican congregations involved in the partnership, statistics show some to be growing, some declining and some inconclusive in terms of their attendance, for a multitude of demographic reasons. Collectively, however, the church was pursuing growth in ways that each isolated congregation might not be able.

Being a presence in every community also requires courageous commitment to places where this is less easy. A bishop interviewed in the preliminary stage spoke about the need to put this into practice by continuing to resource ministry where it is hardest:

> *The strength of the Church of England has been to have priests living alongside the poor in those places... The church we're supposed to be, the Church of England, is one that covers all those places regardless of whether people can pay or not, keeping a presence in every community.*

It is not innately harder to grow a church in a more deprived parish and the statistics do not indicate a correlation between deprivation and growth. However, when growth occurs, it is portrayed as being hard won in these parishes. We heard about one priest working "heroically" in a difficult outer estate parish who has had his "confidence knocked" because everything he has tried has worked reasonably well, but "without seeing the flourishing we're presented with in other places."

If a church building closes, however necessarily, it is perceived not only as the church leaving a place but also as God leaving a place. In one case study, an estate parish in a deprived and geographically isolated coastal community, we heard how one by one, the churches of other denominations had closed and left the area. The Roman Catholic Church there had held its last Mass the same week we visited. That the Anglican Church remained was not in itself evidence of flourishing, but had strengthened the resolve of the congregation to continue worshipping and engaging in social action there so that the whole community would know they were still loved by God and his people.

To see the church grow here might involve sacrificial strategic decisions to keep churches open in places where they can't afford to be, or where they don't have many people, in order that there is still a witness in those places. **Pursuing the growth of the church and of the Kingdom in these places might mean actively resourcing churches that are at present declining and funding faithful ministry in tough circumstances in the hope of things changing.**

It is also important for the church to resource the places where people are all the time. In non-commuter areas or areas with high levels of unemployment, what it means to be present to the people in the community is different from in a parish in a dormitory community where people commute out to work during the week. The COVID-19 pandemic has thus far brought changes to working life and the extent to which that is permanent remains to be seen. If these dynamics shift completely, so too will the implications of the ministry of being present to people.

Both growth and social action are often seen as the result of greater connection to the local community, whether through formal partnership or informal relationship.

In one example, a pioneer congregation had been planted in an area of the parish where the church had previously been relatively inactive. One of the first steps in this was developing a working relationship with the 'Friends of the Park' group, known as one of the most active community organisations locally. This group met on Sunday mornings to tend to the park adjacent to the church building and also to socialise; for example, they organised regular litter-picks followed by sharing refreshments. Rather than competing with this, the church decided that the new congregation would meet on Sunday afternoon and the church members would also join in with the park activities. This led to a thriving partnership between the church and the park group, several of whom joined the church. At Christmas, the church was invited to lead the park carol service.

The pioneer minister described how:

> There's a real sense that [the park group] know where we're coming from and are respectful of that. Some of them are on the fringes of church. Those big conversations are there and things about the fifth mark of mission, care of creation – we've spoken about that and why we're passionate about it... There's a general recognition that these community partners are coming from different places with different focuses but actually a shared passion for this land and this community.

In several other case studies, working with local residents' associations was highlighted as being key to engaging locally, and the relationships that had developed in this way had led to new people joining the congregation. It is a visible and constructive way that the church can be seen as active in, with and for its local community.

In the qualitative phase, conducted prior to the pandemic, a small number of participants mentioned the importance of online presence. This was mainly discussed with reference to local community Facebook pages, which are important to community life. Those who mentioned this felt that it was valuable for the church to be present and contributing to the conversation of the local community wherever it takes place, including on social media. These pages were noted as a forum in which needs could be identified that the church might contribute to addressing. Several church leaders gave examples of initiatives or pieces of informal social action that would not have happened without the connections made in these forums, but which had led to the growth of the church community.

In light of the pandemic and the resulting turn to online rather than in-person worship for a season, this is a valuable reminder **that the church's presence in the community can and does extend beyond the physical building.** The way worship happens has necessarily changed and, for some, so has the way the church is able to interact with its community. However, greater engagement with online spaces both for worship and relationship need not only be a consequence of the pandemic, but also a chance for the church to broaden its network in a permanent way.

Engaging in social action is not likely to lead to growth, numerical or spiritual, if no one knows it is happening, and therefore the visible presence of the church is fundamental to its growth. This is not a call for social action to be self-serving or the church advertising for its own sake the good that it does. Rather, it reflects Jesus' words in Matthew 5 about letting the light of the world shine before others that they might see good deeds and glorify God. Where we observed churches growing as a result of their social action, it was also the case that those we

The streets of East Swindon, known as Parks, are empty on a blustery autumn morning. A few mothers lead toddlers past shuttered shops. Two young people stand and chat outside a house, wearing onesies.

Forty per cent of children in Parks are living in poverty, according to a report in 2019. Since then, the main local employer, Honda, has announced the closure of its factory in 2021, and the coronavirus has hit.

"The main problem is one of hopelessness," says the Revd Lydia Morey, the church curate. "There's everything associated with poverty, hunger and lack of job opportunities.

"When the Honda factory announced that it was closing, it was completely devastating, and then the coronavirus came."

The church, she says "is small with limited capacity" but is consistently involved in "building community" and trying to meet the needs of the people in the area. "There is a constant stream of people asking for foodbank vouchers."

A community choir – the Lionesses – was established at the church two-and-a-half years ago. "I think singing lifts your spirits and makes you feel joyful," says the Revd Morey.

The choir's leader is 59-year-old Diane, a mother-of-four who lives with her partner in East Swindon. Abused by her stepfather as a teenager, Diane says she has found "peace" at St John's.

"I have learned that if I need someone to talk to there's always someone to talk to here," she says. "If I need to sit and think, I can. I'm in a different place now. I don't get angry anymore. I would have stood and had a fight before. Now, I would rather walk away." And she is "the most proudest person" of the choir's achievements, which have included singing carols in the nearby Morrison's.

Her best friend, Rose (56) is also a choir member. Rose experienced violence at the hands of her first husband. The church and the choir have changed her, she says.

"This place has been transformational for me. I was scared. Before, I kept myself to myself. Now I like talking to people. It's brought me a long, long way."

encountered outside of the worshipping community actively recognised the church as a positive presence locally.

Questions to consider

— What does the presence of the church look like in your community? What might the presence of the building convey to the community around?

— Does the community know you are present? What could you do to make your presence more visible?

— What are the opportunities and the challenges of the physical presence of the church where you are?

b. Perseverance

If the church's community presence remains important despite declining national affiliation, the perseverance and long-term nature of this presence is a key reason why.

The stories people tell about their community often go back several decades, or even centuries, and reflect the continued presence of the church throughout that history. The community may have experienced mixed socioeconomic fortunes over that period and the congregation may also have struggled. **The history of a place is often tied to the history of the church in ways that are deeply rooted in local culture.** For example, if a neighbourhood was built around a particular industry that has now gone, the community may have lost something of its identity. However, unlike the mine, steelworks or other emblem of decline local people point to, the church has stayed put.

When the reverse is true, this is felt by the whole community. In one parish where there had historically been a high turnover of clergy, congregation members and local residents alike spoke about how their whole community was framed as a place that no one wanted to stay and that it takes time for the hurt of that to heal. Another vicar told us:

> *When I came sixteen years ago, someone said to me 'you will stay, won't you?' and I didn't understand what they meant... I am the longest serving vicar by a huge margin. The church had been open fifty years and the average stay was less than five years.*

The local church has the potential to build social and spiritual capital by bucking these narratives, but may also entrench them further by mirroring the community's decline.[2]

Particularly in more deprived communities, the long-term presence of the church contrasts starkly with the approach of statutory organisations and charities, which may only work in the area for a short time then leave when the initiative's funding changes. This is true not only of finances but also individual people. **The church can represent consistent community leadership of the sort not always enjoyed by other groups or institutions**. For example, one vicar noted that their seven years of incumbency made them the longest standing community leader in the parish. Another priest we interviewed had been in the post for five years and had worked with four different head teachers in the local primary school in that time, telling us:

> *We don't want to be like everyone else who comes and go. Part of the fruits of the spirit is to be long-suffering and patient. That's part of the Holy Spirit working in people... The biblical narrative is a long-term thing, not a quick in-and-out turnaround.*

The Greek word typically translated as 'patience' in the context of the fruits of the spirit – *makrothumia* – has connotations of endurance and 'long-sufferingness' not only of patiently waiting for something, and this is an important dimension for the church to focus on collectively.

In these scenarios, the church has the capacity to bring different agencies together and share its institutional knowledge. People in places that have experienced this high level of turnover in social workers, teachers, councillors and other community workers may be reluctant to build relationship and trust because of the perception that people will continue to come and go. The parish model means that church leadership and most of those who volunteer within the church live within the community, which is an asset not necessarily shared by statutory agencies or charities. The value and stability of the church, as one congregation member and resident in an estate parish said, is that "we are there, we live there and we don't go home at the end of the day".

One of the catalysts for the turnover of community stakeholders is short-term funding cycles, with local council funding having been reduced significantly in the last decade.[3] **Where some people lament that the state has taken over much of the social function of the church, the gift of the church has always been that it will endure beyond the current iteration of state funding.** A fear expressed by a number of participants was that, at the same time that local churches are trying to shift their community work away from reliance on short-term funding (e.g. lottery funding) because of its lack of sustainability, the central church institution and the Church Commissioners are perceived as moving towards short-termism in their financial structures.

One priest we interviewed, in an outer estate parish, explained his theory that the waves of fortune experienced by a community are mirrored by the church, but with a delay.

The parish had been a desirable place to live when it was first built as a garden estate on the edge of the city centre, but over several decades since has gained a degree of notoriety and a bad reputation. The church has, it seems, echoed the decline of the community. There had not been an incumbent for almost five years before the current vicar was appointed, which had had a profound effect on the congregation. The advert for the vacancy described a 'desperate' community with 'significant problems'. Three of the four parishes in the benefice that spans the estate have congregations that are small and in decline, and all four are in the 5% most deprived parishes nationally.[4]

> *The churches have been on that same wave, but as the churches always are, we're a wave behind or half a wave behind. As the community went down, we went down as well and we've not come up yet properly, but there are signs of growth.*

For this priest therefore, the apparent decline of the parish church might not be cause for undue desperation, but rather part of the natural cycle of local community fortunes. The estate itself is beginning to recover but while the church is active and well known in the community, it has not yet reversed the trend of declining attendance. However, the worshipping community is 75% larger than the parish's usual Sunday attendance, and it is growing. These 'signs of growth' are primarily from midweek acts of worship for local families and food bank guests.

The church as a body of people may be subject to the same ups-and-downs present in the lives of its congregation. There is however a critical role for the church in telling a more positive story and effective lasting transformation. In as much as social action leads to the flourishing of the whole community, it can also be seen to lead to the flourishing of the church itself. This recalls the words of Jeremiah 29:7 about "seeking the peace and prosperity of the city to which I have carried you into exile. Pray to the Lord for it, because if it prospers, you too will prosper." Social action is a way of the church effecting this. Coupled with a focus on praying for the community in ways which may deepen discipleship too, this is seen to lead to growth.

The longevity of the church not only means that the church intends to remain in a place for the long haul, but also that it is prepared to persevere and invest in processes and relationships that will take a long time to develop. The result of this is that the growth of the church may therefore appear slow. Analogies of sowing seeds, tending plants and waiting were frequently used by interviewees and are also central to many of Jesus' parables of kingdom growth. Implicit in these agricultural metaphors is the understanding that growth naturally takes time and perseverance. **The sustained and sustainable growth of a congregation** – what we might call good growth – **takes time, especially when it arises from social action** and engagement with vulnerable communities.

As one community worker on an outer estate told us:

I'm learning that it's not about quick fixes. Some things take a long time. It's been seven years but we're only just beginning to see the fruit. It's taken five, six years to put that foundation down. It's hard when people expect quick wins because it's not like that in this context at all.

One case study church on an estate had recently established a new congregation on a Sunday afternoon. This service is more informal than the traditional worship of the Sunday morning congregation and consists of over 50 adults and children, most of whom did not worship at the church previously. The service is not only attended but also led by local residents including single parents and individuals with long-term health problems, who have grown in faith and been empowered in leadership even before they were confirmed or committed members of the church.

When we visited, the congregation had only been running for a matter of months, but was already thriving. Statistically speaking, many of the individuals would be counted as part of the church for the first time that year. However, the vicar felt it would feel somewhat "disingenuous" to claim a growth of 50 people in just one year. She noted that the relationships within the community, which had given rise to the new congregation, had taken years to build, through community activities including a parenting course, community choir and regular coffee mornings as well as through the informal processes of living in the parish and getting to know people over several years. The new congregation itself was just the tip of the iceberg.

Many of the activities run by churches within their community, such as those listed by the vicar here, are not perceived as part of congregational growth. However, growth in relationships through these activities may be a precursor to church growth in a more recognisable sense; what we might describe as 'pre-growth'. The point at which people began attending a worshipping congregation – and therefore register in the church's statistics – may actually be a long way along their journey of discipleship and relationship with the church.

Statistical measures of church growth that equate the church with the weekly congregation belie the groundwork and investment in someone's life prior to this point. Similarly, the church may in fact be growing long before its growth registers in attendance figures.

Returning to the agricultural metaphor, one interviewee illustrated this by describing the point at which a plant or crop breaks through the earth. This is not the point at which the plant actually begins growing, nor the point at which the work of the grower begins. It is merely the point at which the long-term growth of the plant in putting down roots becomes visible above the ground. Similarly, the point at which church growth is visible in numbers is not necessarily the point at which the church begins to grow nor the point where the work begins.

The same imagery may be applied not only to congregational growth, but also to individual growth in faith and discipleship. The point at which a person professes to be a follower of Jesus, or a disciple, is not also a point of dramatic conversion at the very beginning of their faith story. More commonly, their journey begins far earlier and more gently, but the sustained presence and attention of the church over that time contributes to the growth that emerges.

Some forms of church social action by their very nature encourage longevity of relationship. Involvement in parent and toddler groups, for example, typically lasts several years because children progress through them. A parent with multiple children might have been in a sustained relationship with the local church for 5-10 years by the time their youngest child reaches school age, or longer still if there is a church primary school in the parish.

In three different case study parishes, campaigning work to keep local primary schools open when they were threatened with closure was described as an important piece of social action. None of them was a church-affiliated primary school, but the church and its members recognised the shared community institutional identity and the importance of sustaining it. Through this, the church can retain social capital in a place. If the church was formative in their childhood, people remember it fondly and come back for occasional offices. One case study vicar has been in the parish for seventeen years and now finds himself marrying couples he knew as young children in the toddler group when he arrived, or baptising the children of children he had baptised over a decade earlier. This is particularly apparent in communities with relatively little population churn; it is important that the specific local church was the significant point of engagement, not just the church at large.

Perseverance, not only longevity, is therefore a contributing factor to growth. It is paramount that the church is actively present in a sustained way for its community, over time, not just that it remains there. As the previous section highlighted, the nature of the church's presence is as influential as the fact of it. The sustainability of this presence ought not to be taken for granted, and is perhaps a laurel on which the Church of England as an institution has rested too easily for too long. It is vital not to be naïve about the challenge of sustaining ministry, including in a financial sense.

As attendance figures continue to decline, there are implications for the financial and physical sustainability of the church. In 2019, 25% of parishes counted 14 or fewer people in their usual Sunday attendance.[5] Even with a more optimistic view than the narrative of inevitable decline, this is a significant proportion of parishes that are teetering towards a congregation size which cannot justify or sustain a building or independent presence. The parishes in this size bracket are disproportionately rural, representing a large number of old, isolated church buildings that are as much of a burden as they are a blessing to the church.

There are clearly some significant challenges to the resourcing and financing of ministry. During the COVID-19 pandemic, several dioceses placed numbers of diocesan staff and in some cases even members of the clergy on furlough, in order to make financial savings. One diocese has already announced plans to reduce its stipendiary clergy by almost 25% in the next 18 months, bringing forward reforms that were planned to take four years in an indication that the pandemic had put pressure on already squeezed diocesan finances.[6]

Previous research found that growth is correlated with stipendiary clergy.[7] It is easier to grow a church with a full-time incumbent vicar and the leadership an individual can provide to the whole community is invaluable, but it is paradoxically harder to resource this level of ministry without sufficient congregational growth to fund it. This represents a challenge for many dioceses, which are forced to square uncertain finances with the need for ministry. Once again, the economic situation ahead is likely to be challenging, and the Church of England is not immune from that – nor from the difficult decisions it may necessitate.

However, longevity cannot lead to complacency, nor does it mean ministry is immutable. It is easy to think that because the church has always been here, it always will be, but this is not inherently the case. In one rural parish, many long-standing members of the congregation spoke about how they had felt they didn't need to engage in a community listening process encouraged by the diocese, because they had been there long enough to know the community well already. However, it transpired that some of their impressions of the parish were years out of date and they were surprised by how much they learned. The congregation had become disconnected from the parish community and found it helpful to take stock of that.

There are different timelines of growth and discipleship to recognise. In some contexts, while the church is an enduring presence, its involvement in individuals' lives may be more short-term by virtue of their circumstances. In student ministry, for example, time is of the essence and the church might 'only' have three years to disciple someone within the congregation. Similarly, and in an even shorter term, specific churches engaging with asylum seekers and refugees might only have contact with someone for a matter of months before they are moved on to live somewhere else. In both these contexts, the church is seen as "the people who stay and stay and stay, and disciple and disciple and disciple," regardless of how many people pass through the congregation and move on. In these cases, creativity in discipleship is important. One church leader spoke about having adapted their baptism preparation course to allow it to be completed in under six weeks – the amount of time an asylum seeker would typically be in the parish before being rehoused.

The longevity and perseverance of the church is not necessarily at odds with the transience of individual lives. **The church's long-term presence in a place means it can embody the soul of the place in a way other institutions might not.** For transient populations struggling with an entry point or connection to community, this sense of stability and home might be essential for them however long they are there. The emotional security this engenders then makes them more likely to engage with the church elsewhere, making the church an enduring presence in their lives. The hospitality and acceptance individuals receive from one particular church can make them more disposed to join another church when they move on. This can lead to the growth of the church at large, but requires a more expansive view of growth in order to reflect that.

The value placed here on longevity should not be seen to undermine the potential of Fresh Expressions, new congregations or church plants to grow in places the church has not been embedded over the years. There is a level of faithfulness in having kept something going for a long time that is a different dynamic to the equally significant faith of starting something new. Within the mixed ecology of the church, both are valuable and both have their place.

Questions to consider

— What does 'perseverance' means in your community?

— Where and how does your church/congregation enjoy the benefits of its long-term commitment to the community?

— Where and how might you seek to develop this further?

c. Hospitality

When a church has a strong culture of hospitality and welcome as the norm, its approach to social action is necessarily changed and the church is able to flourish.

Social action does not inherently lead to the growth and discipleship of those involved, but with the right culture, it has the potential to do both those things. A study of non-religious individuals in the USA found that one of the top predictive factors of growing churches was their hospitality to the unchurched.[8] The theologian Chris Allen argues that radical hospitality rather than transactional forms of aid is the correct

Bosede is a 47-year-year old single mum with a 17-year-old daughter. She received support from St John's Church in Hoxton when she and her daughter became homeless, and is now exploring the idea of ordination.

"My dad died and I lost my job. Because I lost my job, I lost my flat. We went to a homeless hostel. It was awful. It was degrading. I was sad. It was depressing. I don't know how I survived that, but I did. I was worried for my daughter.

"We went into the hostel in the January and I never forget that day in March. I was in church and someone offered to pray with me. Then I got a call immediately saying that I could view a flat. Everyone screamed! We moved in on 1 April 2015.

"I am grateful to everyone who prayed for me during that time. Today, I'm happy and I can say that it was a miracle. My daughter talks about it too and says it's our miracle flat. She's studying for her A levels now and I couldn't be more proud.

"Now, I'm helping people who are going through what I went through. My vicar leads them to me if they have housing problems, or someone needs prayer. God prepared me ahead of time for that.

"I'm exploring the idea of ordination. It's taken me almost ten years to make up my mind to do that. But now, I'm in the process. It's scary, but I pray it all goes well."

theological posture of the church in response to food poverty.[9] There is a profound difference between feeding someone and eating with them. The exchange of a food parcel, for example, does not innately welcome a person into the life of the church, nor does it innately deepen the faith of the volunteer.

To consider a concrete example, food banks are acknowledged as "deeply contradictory spaces in which [people] can feel great shame or express real agency; in which volunteers can be hardened by their exposure to suffering or softened by the stories they hear."[10] The difference between shame/suffering and agency/softening here is not a practical difference in the running of the food bank – the material purpose of the space remains the same – but a difference of attitude and intention. It can also mean the same space is experienced differently, depending on an individual's role as guest or host, volunteer or organiser.

Without an intentional culture of hospitality, social action in any form can remain purely transactional rather than transformative for the entire church community.

With the right change in culture, existing congregations and their activities can become more hospitable and grow through doing so. After a succession of changes in leadership, parishioners in one case study, where the church building was on a busy high street, recognised a need to develop a greater sense of community. Through listening to local people, both inside and outside of the church, they found that loneliness and isolation was a significant problem for people in the town. There was a small midweek congregation of about 10-15 people who gathered for coffee and fellowship after the service. The church decided to develop this informal coffee slot into a Place of Welcome, opening the church doors and offering free hot drinks, soup and toast for anyone who would like it, whether or not they attended the service beforehand.

This has grown so much that the church has had to buy extra tables and chairs to accommodate everybody who comes; an average of 40 people come each week. It is a buzzing hub of conversation, where friendships have developed and the church has become known as somewhere welcoming where people can come for a hot drink and a chat, whatever their circumstances. This parish attendance, which was previously declining, is now deemed inconclusive, suggesting that the downward trend has begun to be reversed.

If social action is to lead to congregational growth and discipleship, it is vital that the ethos of hospitality is consistent throughout everything the community does. If there is a discrepancy between the welcome someone might receive at a midweek social action project and the welcome that might be extended to the same individual on a Sunday morning, for example, it is harder for them to move from beneficiary to disciple. To return to the 'voices of theology' model, if the espoused theology of a church and its operant theology of its social action differ in their approach to hospitality, this may hinder spiritual or numerical growth.[11]

Similarly, if the content of a church's preaching does not reflect the importance of generous service in the community, it is harder to integrate social action fully with the life of the church. In one case study parish, the clergy spoke about the cultural change of consciously preaching with the expectation that the congregation consisted of food bank guests, not just better off volunteers. This was described as an eye-opener for some of the more comfortable members of the congregation, but the leadership felt it had been crucial for the growth of the church:

> *For most of our people, it's not an issue for them. We've definitely made that effort to talk about it. Within our own congregation, there is a family who share two rooms with two other families and rely on the food bank. That's in our church – it's about trying to get people to see that.*

In addition to the material importance of physically feeding people, eating together can help churches create a space of intentional relationship and the sharing of food is often at the core of church social action. However, this activity alone does not automatically grow the church. 86% of Anglican churches are involved in some way with the provision of lunch clubs, coffee mornings or similar initiatives.[12] 53% are involved in other forms of community cafés not targeted at a specific demographic and yet not all of these are growing numerically.

The way we offer hospitality has the potential to shift power dynamics within a community, beginning to dissolve existing social categories, but can also strengthen these divides. It can be an opportunity for the church to challenge societal notions of class and privilege, for example, forging a community of equality in contrast to the contemporary culture and economy.

There might be different tables of fellowship shared by the church community, with different circles of inclusion and standards of hospitality applied to each. For example, in the course of a week, the same church community could play host to a communion table, a congregational bring-and-share, a community café and a night shelter meal for rough sleepers, but the groups of people who are welcome at each of these might vary. Implicit social norms within the congregation can make it harder for people to move between these. We might argue, however, that in a church where the three aspects of growth, relationship and action were well integrated, these tables and what they represent would start to become indistinguishable from each other.

This is not always unproblematic. Breaking down these categories requires something of the congregation and a transfer of power relations in a way that may feel difficult or uncomfortable. One vicar expressed the challenge of this:

> *The dynamic of what it means to embrace people in a sense of hospitality theologically and to think about the dynamic of who is host and who is guest is hard. Co-hosting might be something that takes a lot more work because you've got to find a radical space, a brave space where two different sets of people – new and old – can actually start to walk together at the same pace which is a new pace to what's been set before. They start to speak a language that's new to both of them.*

This can mean speaking a shared language of collective worship as well as social action. In several of the case study parishes, we observed the ways in which growing congregations blur the lines between social action and worship, in particular around food. The shared table and the meal eaten together transcend the sometimes binary categories of social action and discipleship.

One parish church, for example, holds a midweek 'Agape' service, where the congregation sits at tables laid out around a central table with a loaf of bread, which is prayed over and then handed round the tables to be eaten with hot bowls of soup. After the meal, there is a short reflection on the day's gospel reading and a collection plate is passed around for those who are able to contribute to buying the soup for the following week. It is not a Eucharist service in name or in formal liturgy, nor is it pure social action devoid of spiritual content, but it is recognisably an act of worship, focused on a meal shared by a gathered congregation – many of whom are not part of the Sunday congregation and whose faith has grown and discipleship taken place primarily through their attendance on Wednesday lunchtimes. This church is growing by all metrics, but the growth of the worshipping community and average weekly attendance is more marked than that of the usual Sunday attendance, reflecting the importance of activities such as the Agape service.

In another case study, in a more deprived part of a city generally perceived as prosperous, interviewees spoke about how there is "an act of worship attached to every act of hospitality" in their community. Throughout the week, the church hosts various different meals that draw in often vulnerable members of the local community and there is an optional service alongside each of these. This might be as simple as a short service of candle lighting and prayer before the community lunch club. While these are not enforced, it emphasises the connection between different aspects of church life. Of those who come to the lunch club and accompanying service, not all would articulate a Christian faith and only a minority ever attend Sunday worship at the church. However, according to the vicar, the midweek visit to the church is, for some, "the only place they are loved, feel safe and belong," which is attributed to the worship element as well as the meal itself. The worshipping community of this church is nearly double the size of its usual Sunday attendance. While the Sunday attendance here is inconclusive, the average weekly attendance – which includes several of the optional services that run in parallel with the parish's social action – is seen to be growing.

In another church with a strong Eucharistic tradition, people spoke about the desire to build a kitchen facility in the body of the church building so that the worship space and the thriving community meals could be better integrated. In explaining why this was important for the community, one interviewee here quoted the German liberation theologian Dorothee Sölle, who wrote that, "we should eat more at the Eucharist and we should pray more when eating" and articulated this as being at the heart of the vision of growth for their church.

The theologian and environmentalist Norman Wirzba suggests that the fact Jesus regularly ate with strangers and outcasts is an indication that our fellowship too should be "for the nurture of others and not simply for self-enhancement", to disciple those within and without the community of the church.[13] The imagery and symbolism that Christians attach to bread in particular also sets the church apart from other charitable organisations or 'service providers'. The sharing of a meal is rooted in something more than the simple provision of food to satisfy a need.

As one congregation member we interviewed said:

When we gather around the table and break bread together, that's our go-to image for hospitality and generosity and change and transformation. It's something other organisations wouldn't have.

The Anglican Eucharistic Prayer includes the line, "though we are many, we are one body, because we all share in one bread." The word 'because' in this prayer is critical. It echoes

what Paul writes in 1 Corinthians 10 v 17, the passage the
prayer is drawn from; "because there is one loaf, we, who
are many, are one body, for we all share the one loaf." The
causality implied by the word 'because' suggests that the
loaf itself is instrumental in creating the unity of the body,
rather than simply incidental to the sharing it facilitates.
This is important for the way we view the sharing of food and
hospitality through social action, as well as its implications for
growth and discipleship.

Several participants independently referenced *Take This
Bread*, a theological memoir by American writer Sara Miles as
being influential on their thinking about what it means to feed
people in the context of church.[14] In it, Miles tells the story of
her journey from atheism to faith through encountering the
community of the church and in particular, the sacrament
of bread and wine. The transformation she experienced in
coming to faith led her into establishing food pantries for those
in material poverty in her city, directly illustrating the link
between discipleship and action.

The food – and not just the fact that we share it – is an
expression of unity and community. **The spirit in which it is
shared is also important if the church is to grow and flourish; it
must be characterised by radical hospitality**.

More widely, the growth of Messy Church, a
congregational model engaging in mission and discipleship
with largely unchurched children and families, is an example
of this. Food is one of the central elements of Messy Church
and is embedded in the structure of the service in a way that
traditional congregations do not do. Neither those attending
it nor those running it use the language of "staying for a meal
afterwards"; it is seen as a core aspect of the congregational

life of Messy Church, rather than the part that happens when the other activities have finished. Although the Messy Church model is not universally successful, in many places it has developed as a congregation in its own right. At their best, there are examples of Messy Churches growing numerically at a far greater pace than the Sunday congregation as well as going deeper in discipleship. Church Army research found that 81% of Messy Church leaders say they have seen evidence of lives changed in some way by being a part of it and 21% of Messy Church congregations have held baptisms.[15]

Hospitality is also about making church accessible to the whole community, both in terms of everyone being able to access worship and also being aware how culture affects this. A culture of hospitality within the church does necessarily mean that every member is comfortable hosting a dinner party, but rather that it is understood as important in their context.

One individual we interviewed suggested that in a welcoming church community, it would be natural to invite newcomers to join you for lunch. They implied it would be a negative indication of church cultures were that not the case.

> We've started doing a series of dinners in people's homes, which is just about people getting to know each other. You could do that in any church couldn't you? It's not revolutionary.

In other parishes, however, people talked about how inviting people to your own home for a meal was simply not the social norm in their wider community and so congregation members would not be quick to do so. What is "not revolutionary" and may be helpful to the growth of the church community in a middle-class context used to hosting may be alien to other contexts, as we heard, and this has implications for discipleship models as well as social action.[16]

There are, however, creative ways of instilling the same spirit in a culturally and practically relevant way. One church has grown a pioneer congregation centred on eating Sunday lunch together in a community space on their housing estate, allowing the community to share collectively in the hospitality of a meal. Another church has designated a 'living room' space in their church building, with sofas and a television, where people can host 'house groups' for discipleship in a neutral but comfortable space without the pressure of it being literally in their own house.

Hospitality is historically part of the church. The fact that Jesus ate with people is an oft-repeated model, as is the importance of sharing and eating together in the growth and formation of the early church in the book of Acts. It is also an important part of the heritage of individual church communities and one that is valuable to rediscover.

One member of the clergy in a small rural town spoke about how their church building had first been established eight hundred years ago as a *hospitium*, or place of hospitality, connected to the neighbouring Benedictine monastery. In the Middle Ages, this was a cross between a hospital, a hospice and a hostel, all of which share the same etymology in the Latin word *hospitium*. Strangers and pilgrims might have come there to receive an unconditional welcome and to be fed, cared for and in some cases to die in the sacred space. Hospitality was in the foundational vision of the parish church in that town and the rector suggested that there was "something implicit within this place, in the air almost, and when the church lives up to that vision, it thrives". The growth and discipleship of the congregation in recent years has been closely connected with seeking to live up to that vision and reignite the spirit of hospitality that was part of their church's origins.

Through hosting a food bank, members of the congregation came to know a man who had been sleeping rough in the town. A local councillor brought him to the church when he had nowhere to sleep, because of the reputation of the church as somewhere to find help. He came to live in the church for over three months, with members of the church community supporting him. Many in the wider community were also drawn in by the story and donated food and money to the church; some visited the church for the first time or the first time in a long time in order to do so. This, we were told, mirrors the vision of the building and faith community as a *hospitium*, with hospitality at its core in the same way that would have been true for the monastic community of the thirteenth century.

> *He was actually living here in the church, sleeping in a pew, over the Christmas period so there was this enormous challenge for us of thinking about 'no room at the inn' when there was someone living in our church who we were feeding.*

Shortly after leaving the church building and being rehoused locally, the man sadly passed away but the church raised enough money to give him a basic funeral. This was attended by over forty church members, who recognised him as a valuable part of their community and someone who had been instrumental in their own faith journey. The story was recounted by several interviewees as something that had deepened their faith in ways they had not expected.

> *We've all been on a journey to recognising that church is not just a place for respectable people, and learning what it looks like to see the presence of Jesus in the flesh of the poor.*

Through modelling to the whole community what Jesus would have done, the congregation encountered Jesus in a

← POST OFFICE
← HAIRCARE
← THE NINETY-NINER S

NOW OPEN

Rose is 56, the eighth of ten children. The mother-of-four fled her home in Birmingham to escape domestic violence. She lives in Swindon with her second husband and attends St John's Church.

"My husband was violent towards me. Because we was married, it was hard to get it sorted. I fled in the middle of the night with my four children. The youngest was 4. The oldest was 11.

"I came to Swindon. I couldn't have contact with my family in case he came after me. I wanted to go to church, but at first, I went in and came straight out again. I met someone called Julie who made me feel calm and welcome here. I brought my children here. I met my second husband.

"They asked me if I wanted to get involved doing things in the church. I started doing tea and coffee and cleaning the toilets. Now I'm a churchwarden.

"My mind was all over the place. I was scared. But I can shout at God now. I can talk now. I never had a voice before. I've learned about myself and about people. I became more happier and kinder to people. Before, I kept myself to myself. Now I like talking to people.

"If you haven't been through hard times, you can't understand people who are going through them. But I know. I understand. I will always point people to where they can get help.

"This place has been transformational for me. I grew up without being a Christian. It's not about the religion, it's about the faith. It's brought me a long, long way."

deeper way. The church has grown stronger and their faith has been strengthened individually and collectively by this practical example of generosity. If discipleship is about cultivating the ways and behaviours of Jesus, then learning generosity through housing a homeless man in the church is an intentional act of discipleship.

Questions to consider

— Where and how does your church offer hospitality to others?

— How do you think the culture of your church might help or hinder this, and what can you do practically to change this?

— How does your theological understanding affect/shape how you think about hospitality?

d. Adaptability

Where the church is growing and flourishing through involvement in social action, the congregation's capacity to adapt and embrace complexity is critical.

The lives and experiences of individuals and communities are not homogeneous, and therefore neither are individual and collective journeys of faith. The circumstances that may have led a person to engage with the church's social action might also have implications for their discipleship and the life of the church, in ways that can challenge the status quo of the church community. This can be an opportunity rather than a barrier for the growth of the church, but requires a level of resilience and compassion within the church.

Neither growth nor discipleship are linear processes by nature. In the same way that the growth of a congregation can be understood through metaphors of natural growth, which convey the time, depth and intentionality required to grow something, the intricacy of individual faith journeys can also be seen in these terms. A linear understanding of growth in terms of church attendance also does not distinguish between the complexities of different individual journeys.

One person described how in their parish, "it's not always a nice, easy trajectory where people come to faith and commit and that's that." They were speaking with respect to the particular challenges of a deprived estate context, but we might question whether it is ever that nice and easy in any context, irrespective of socioeconomic profile.

Another interviewee contrasted the growth of a cedar tree with that of a mustard bush in order to illustrate the diversity and complexity of growth, both individual and congregational. The cedar tree is tall and straight and therefore its growth becomes quickly apparent. The mustard bush grows in a more tangled fashion, growing in length and complexity without appearing much taller like the cedar. It was suggested that if the entwined branches of the mustard plant were stretched out to their full length, they would reach as tall as a cedar tree, but would be less likely to be recognised as such. This was presented as an opportunity for ministry, as well as a challenge to the way we quantify growth and discipleship, which are not always tidy or linear processes.

Social action brings the church into relationship with people whose life stories are less tidy than some corners of the church might be used to.

Echoing Jesus' words that it is "not the healthy who need a doctor, but the sick",[17] one interviewee described their church as being like a hospital, where "nobody in the whole congregation, including the vicarage, was OK". In communities where mental health difficulties, unemployment or dysfunctional family situations are common, the fact that that members of the local church also struggle with these issues can be a healthy sign that the congregation is connected with and representative of its context. Conversely, it might be seen as greater cause for concern if a congregation was not also wrestling with some of the same problems as the wider parish population.

Reductive understandings of discipleship that equate coming to faith with middle-class notions of morality risk missing the complex beauty of some people's experiences. In one case study, we heard the story of an individual for whom the transformative impact of the church in his life was illustrated by the fact that he no longer found himself in situations of running away from the police.

In another case study, a client of the job club run by the church told us:

> *When I first came here, I was bad-tempered and I kept getting wound up. It just didn't end well at all. Doors got broken. Hands got broken. I'd say I was a horrible person. I don't want to swear on your recording, but I was an arsehole. I had the biggest ego and I walked in thinking I was better than everyone else. Now I just think we're all humans loved by God.*

Neither of these individuals are regular members of the Sunday congregation, nor have they made a formal profession of faith. By some definitions, they might not therefore be counted as disciples; "not running away from the police" is not a widely applicable measure of discipleship. Neither would they figure in statistical accounts of church growth. However, there is a transformation of sorts occurring in their lives, attributable in some way to the church, and this might be considered part of a wider journey towards faith, if not yet definitive discipleship. In numerous parishes, people spoke about stories like these and the challenges of integrating them with existing norms of discipleship.

One vicar told this story, noting how it blurred the lines between our research terms:

A lot of people who come to this church have a pattern of broken, damaged or non-existent relationships. We had an alcoholic guy called Jimmy who came here for six years and gave us a lot of grief. We often didn't know what to do with him. But he came Sunday by Sunday and at the second attempt, he moved away and achieved sobriety. When he came back, he actually thanked us and said this was the first place where he'd ever felt he really belonged. I don't know whether you would say that directly falls under the category of social action or discipleship but I think it shows we are building that sense of community.

Many interviewees who have encountered the church through its social action express their faith journey in terms of how their self-perception and behaviour have changed, rather than explicitly how their belief or articulation of their faith has developed. The changes in attitude and behaviour that occur as a person goes deeper in their faith may look different for different people.

In congregations where a large proportion of people have challenging lives, there can be consequences for resources within the church. The word 'complicated' is used frequently in describing people's lives, particularly in more deprived areas. Churches often conceive of money and time as comparable resources for people to give to the church, but for many, neither of these are fully their own to give. For the most economically vulnerable in society, the resource of time is often outside of their control, whether because of shift work, zero hours contracts or caring responsibilities, regardless of whether they would like to commit to a church. Between long working hours, Sunday trading and a culture that prizes busyness, poverty of time, not only of resources, is a reality for many and may restrict their capacity to commit.

As with material poverty though, those who are time poor in the world's terms are not considered poor in kingdom terms, and church communities need to be able to embrace this. Growth here is still valuable, but might not be accompanied by an equivalent growth in capacity.

It can require a great degree of flexibility and adaptability to enable whole congregations to participate fully in the life of church in ways their living circumstances render difficult. Church leaders described the difficulty of dealing with congregation members who often do not know until first thing in the morning whether they will be offered work that day and therefore cannot commit in advance to take on a role in a rota. In one particular congregation in an inner city parish with a large immigrant population and high levels of precarious employment, this applied to a significant proportion of lay leaders. For example, having arranged well in advance to meet with a member of the PCC during a visit to the parish, on the morning of the interview he was called into work at the last minute and was therefore unable to participate.

The church leader explained the logistical challenge this posed:

> My congregation's time isn't always their own, let alone
> ours. It's not that people are inherently unreliable. It's that
> their lives do not allow them to be relied upon, which is really

difficult because you want to plan for someone to bring the bread for communion on Sundays but they might not be there. It's a difficult balancing act as a leader to know whether to do it yourself or to continually try and push it on someone else... when their lives won't allow them.

This congregation has experienced numerical growth to an extent that might not have been possible if it were not adaptable and agile enough to offer to enable individuals like this to participate actively in worship and lay leadership.

Elsewhere, we heard from one individual – a licensed lay reader who works part-time as a care worker – who spoke about how she had had to fight with her employer to be guaranteed Sundays off from her paid work in order to fulfil her role as a reader in the parish. This had come at the cost of agreeing to work early morning and overnight shifts on weekdays, limiting her ability to get involved in the midweek social action activities her church runs.

There is an additional complexity for churches wrestling with the twin pressures of complicated congregations and a societal move away from the sacredness of Sunday as Sabbath. There might be difficulties in extending discipleship and community to those for whom Sunday does not symbolise rest nor an inherently spiritual day of the week, as one curate told us:

It isn't built into family routines here to come to church on Sundays because you've got very fragmented, dysfunctional families. You might have families with one parent in prison. If Mum is a single mum and they go to their dad's on a Sunday, we can't give her what she really needs on that Sunday which is a lie in! It's so difficult to know how you do it.

Furthermore, for many communities, growth can bring with it further challenges for the church. As one lay PCC member acknowledged:

> For us, growing is something that stretches us further rather than resourcing us.

This is hard to articulate without denigrating or patronising those who are joining the church and whose part in the community should be celebrated. However, it is a reality that in many cases, growth increases pastoral challenges. This is particularly hard in churches without large staff teams or administrators where the majority of pastoral care thus falls to the clergy.

In order for the church to embrace growth and adaptability together, there is a need for a degree of congregational resilience and openness to lament. In several case studies, we encountered congregation members wrestling with the sadness of an individual they had invested time and energy into having reoffended or fallen back into addiction. Sometimes they questioned whether the faith and transformation they had celebrated had been genuine, and whether it had been worth it only to experience the ensuing disappointment and grief. This requires a huge amount of emotional resilience and compassion, modelled at every level of church leadership, in order to travel along the whole journey with individuals and show them grace at every stage.

One lay leader spoke emotionally about a young man with whom they had walked part of this journey but who had since returned to prison:

It could have been the biggest success story on earth the way he was going, until he fell back off the wagon, but we're still praying for him.

In a number of case studies, we also heard about the importance of grieving together as a community – a marker of a pastoral approach capable of handling the joys and sorrows of life together. One church with significant outreach to the local homeless community frequently holds funerals for rough sleepers. This was described not only as the extension of the social action work, but also the beginnings of discipleship for those who attend such funerals, often fellow rough sleepers, who are given space and dignity to mourn their friends.

For some congregations, the ability to model within the church the complexity of their community is seen as a strength and a contributing factor to their growth. Where new churches have started with little resource and no physical building, in particular in the estate context, people often respond well to the vulnerability and fragility because they recognise it in their own lives. This is not necessarily replicable where the church is already established.

If the church is recognised as a place where it is acceptable to bring the messiness and complexity of your life and admit when things are difficult, it is more likely to be a place people feel they want to join. This can stem from the honesty and openness of church leaders about their own struggles, sometimes in ways as simple as acknowledging that theirs are the children misbehaving during the service. It can involve interaction within the service and the agility to adapt to people's reactions during worship and the mood of the congregation that particular day.

One church staff member noted that:

> *We don't get called hypocrites by people on the estate because we're open about being failures.*

One case study congregation described having made a deliberate effort to smile at people arriving late to worship rather than tut at them or make them feel uncomfortable, mindful of the myriad reasons why they might not be on time. The collective response to something as simple as arriving late conveys a great deal about the congregation's aptitude to handle complexity. The church leadership can be instrumental in how it models this to the congregation. This is another example of how a church's culture is as influential on its flourishing as the action it engages in.

Whilst the Fresh Expressions model of church is not the focus of this research project, we nonetheless encountered multiple congregations where creative expressions of church were central to the connection of social action with discipleship and ensuing growth; for example, congregations which had grown organically from social action projects. This was not a factor in the sampling process, but in the end around a quarter of the case study parishes had additional congregations that fit this description, not including those which run Messy Church. We observe that these models can enable and equip church communities well to handle complexity.

One church in one of the most deprived parishes nationally began a house group for drug addicts, consisting of a meal and a chance to pray together. From the very start, the model – called Ignite –blurred the lines of social action and discipleship, offering both without condition. This group grew rapidly and the decision was made to run an Alpha Course, which attracted 80-100 people each week. At the end of the course, there was a desire to continue meeting, which led to the establishing of a midweek congregation with "all the hallmarks of church" but aimed at those on the margins of the community.

It was originally an attempt to meet those who were marginalised, who were poorly educated or who had special needs or criminal records, lifestyle challenges and all that malarkey. People who felt sidelined from society and like they might not belong in church or might not be welcome in church. Ours was an intentional attempt to reverse that feeling.

Ten years on, this model has proved successful and been adopted at a diocesan level. Funding has been secured from the Church Commissioners to replicate it in five other marginalised communities across the diocese. The funding covers intentional community engagement, employing lay missioners to build relationships within the community with a view to beginning midweek Ignite congregations following the original pattern.

The worship style is flexible and adaptable, with a high value placed on interaction and no assumptions made about people's literacy or prior understanding of faith. Parallels can be drawn with the Messy Church model, in that the service often includes video content, practical activities and creative ways of praying in addition to a shared meal. It is seen as complementary to rather than competitive with the Sunday congregation. Individuals are able to move between the two if they wish, although this is not emphasised as the ultimate goal, which is rather that people come into a relationship with Jesus in whatever context they find most comfortable.

Standing in the encircling gloom of a wet autumn evening, the Revd Derek Maddox points outside the church and says, "this was all farmland."

It was. Until 1952, this was a rural area of farmland. But then, the farms were compulsorily purchased, and the Hartcliffe area of Bristol was developed, initially around the Imperial Tobacco factory and offices. The factory is long gone, but the extensive council estates remain, home to more than 11,000 people. Hartcliffe is, however, a long way from the fashionable image of much of Bristol. Beset by financial poverty, food poverty, drugs, mental health and debt issues, the life expectancy of someone in Hartcliffe is between 7-10 years less than those in the surrounding city.

St Andrew's Church is trying to meet the needs of the community: and most of those needs revolve around food. A food bank provided seven days' worth of food for 30 people (many of whom represented whole families) each week. Since the coronavirus began, that has tripled to at least 90 people each week.

Just over a year ago, the church opened its doors on a Sunday afternoon, inviting the community in for a hot meal, and a short time of worship and Bible reading. "People would say that they hadn't had a decent hot meal in weeks,' says the priest-in-charge, the Revd Derek Maddox. On a Wednesday night, the church has a "more formal" evening of testimonies, at which end-of-day food from Greggs is given out.

"I felt that we really needed to feed people, because that was the need here," says the Revd Maddox. "We didn't have any expectations of them signing up to be believers. It was about supporting people." But, he adds, "Some people have been mightily touched by God."

One of those is 38-year-old skip driver, BJ. A lifelong drug user and alcoholic, BJ came to faith in 2016. He now helps at the Wednesday evening testimony night. "I haven't even got to speak," he says. "Everyone knows I was a crack cocaine addict, but I've turned my life around. So, the people think that Jesus must be real. I do it because I want to see as many souls as possible in heaven. And I'm seeing it lots, yeah. It's great, great to see. It's mind blowing."

The Saturday Gathering community in Halifax is another example of this model. It grew out of the ecumenical food bank partnership in the town. The leaders recognised that many of the guests were interested in exploring faith but would not be comfortable with the existing congregations, nor were the congregations necessarily in a position to welcome those with serious addiction problems, low literacy or mental health issues. The gathering is flourishing, with over 100 people attending each week, and other congregations have been established in different areas of the town. It meets on a Saturday night, in recognition of this being a time when statutory services are not available and those attending might otherwise struggle. The local police have acknowledged a related reduction in incidents in the town centre at this time.

Unlike the Ignite model, Saturday Gathering is outside of the parish structures; it is an ecumenical gathering rather than an Anglican fresh expression. However, the local parish congregation has grown demonstrably, as have several of the other denominational churches involved. One of the pioneer leaders was a curate at the local parish church and, with the support of the bishop, a number of people have been confirmed in context of the Saturday Gathering. The leadership now includes several individuals who came to faith through the Gathering.

Questions to consider

— What are some of the particular ways your church/ congregation needs to be adaptable?

— How does your church community handle complexity? Sadness? Celebration?

e. Generosity

The generosity of the church, both financially and otherwise, can be a key contributory factor to its growth, particularly when it is expressed as a commitment of faith.

The parameters of the Strategic Development Fund equate growth with financial strength, assuming that a growing congregation will also be a more financially sustainable one. 'Rising giving' is suggested as an indicator of improving discipleship. This is something to aspire to and it is important to encourage generosity as part of the Christian life, but it cannot be assumed that this equation will play out in all contexts. Radical generosity is not dependent on the material wealth of the church or its congregation, but rather its attitude and willingness to take risks in faith. Decisions taken sacrificially in faith, even from a position of apparent financial instability, can lead to growth.

One vicar acknowledged the financial difficulties of their church:

> We haven't got peanuts as a church. We're a congregation of refugees and unemployed people, so we'll never increase the giving massively. I can't rely on the congregation to pay me.

This is not always contingent on the church's capacity to give. For example, in one diocese, a partnership between a wealthy parish and a more deprived parish in the same area thrived for a while when resources of time were shared. However, when the wealthier parish were asked to contribute financially to the resourcing of the poorer parish, the PCC were unwilling and the partnership broke down. We might hope that Christians are more inclined to see giving as part of their discipleship, but that is not always automatically the case, just as it is also true that there are those with deep, committed faith with limited capacity to give.

In one case study, the small and declining congregation had been sustained for many years by the interest on a bequest left in a will by a local resident who wanted to the church to continue. Giving from within the congregation was not sufficient to cover the costs of running the church. At a crossroads regarding the future of the church, the clergy and congregation prayed about what to do. They felt guided by God through discernment to invest the entire legacy fund into renovating the church building, in order to serve their local community better. In addition, they took the decision not to sell off a piece of land adjacent to the church to developers, which would have brought in significant income, but to use that land for community purposes too.

In telling this story, the vicar conveyed how the church's PCC was characterised by its faith and generosity in a way that led them naturally to trust God with finances:

> *Doing the building project meant using all of that money to create a community space and a beautiful worship environment. The PCC was and still is a PCC of faith... That was a big deal, letting go of that security blanket and not being able to trust in that big pot of money but trusting God to provide for what he was telling us to do. But they said, 'We've seen the fruit of what we've done already and we're totally behind the work of the food bank. Let's do it.'*

The building project completed as a result has significantly increased the presence of the church within the community and grown its capacity for social action and hospitality, alongside the numerical growth of the Sunday congregation from 16 to over 40 over a two-year period. Through this, the church has also developed relationships with local organisations who use the new space, which contributes to the continued financial stability of the church.

A longstanding church member told us:

> *It's interesting that when we've taken those steps of faith and trusted God for his provision, he has provided. We would never have imagined being able to get that amount of money... It's been remarkable and God's been great.*

In another case study, congregation members explicitly describe hearing God's vision for their community in the form of a building project they knew should be financially impossible for them. In spite of this, they decided to commit to the project for the benefit of the whole community and have been able to fund it through grants and charitable giving. One interviewee here drew on the biblical example of the Widow's Mite to describe what felt like a numerically small but practically large financial commitment from the congregation resulting in blessing or reward.

> *We have a small church community who are up for doing it and are excited by what on paper shouldn't be possible. Sunday morning attendance is about 70 or 80 and it's not a gathered church so it's made up of people from the immediate area, which is in the 10% most deprived areas in the country. The congregation is made up of people from the immediate area. £2 million just should not be possible but we are well on our way.*

As well as generosity in terms of finance and building resource, we encountered examples of creative generosity between congregations. For example, one parish had "donated" the time of a member of its congregation to act as PCC treasurer for a neighbouring parish. This stemmed from the relationship between the two congregations, and also the recognition that while one had a surfeit of professionals with the capacity to take on the role, the other did not. This exchange increased the practical capacity of the less resourced parish and reduced the pressure on the clergy there, but also deepened the discipleship of the individual in question, who was able to use their gifts to contribute to the life of the church.

Questions to consider

— What are some examples/stories of generosity from your church community?

— Other than financial giving, how might your congregation creatively express generosity to the community?

f. Participation and invitation

A key facet of social action is that it increases the range of ways in which individuals can participate in the church community and thus help it grow. Not only might they take part in worship, but they are enabled to contribute to the life of the church through volunteering at other activities. Through this, people grow in their discipleship and the church grows bigger, deeper and stronger. In the stories that they tell of participation in worship, central to their experience of the church community, interviewees often connect belonging with active participation through, for example, being asked to take part in the offertory or help serve coffee after the service.

The CGRP found that strong lay leadership is connected with growth.[18] The lack of lay involvement is also correlated within decline, whether this is because the congregation aren't willing to get involved or because they aren't permitted to do so. This shows that a culture of permission giving between clergy and laity is important, but so is an approach to discipleship that encourages the laity to see involvement in social action and worship as part of their faith. Growth arises not only from empowering and inviting lay people to participate in all aspects of church life, but also from helping them to view it as essential for their discipleship. Social action is instrumental in this in that expands the ways in which lay people can become involved in church life.

In interviews, volunteers often articulate their reasons for becoming involved in a particular social action project or activity as beginning with the fact that they were asked to take part, rather with than the moment their theological thinking crystallised and they understood the Christian importance of doing it. For some, this is in the form of a congregational invitation – for example, a mention in the church notices that more volunteers were wanted – while for others, it is a personal invitation. This is not to say that they do not have a faith motivation underpinning their involvement, but rather that being asked was a significant catalyst for them.

One individual who had been part of the congregation for many years emphasised the importance of personal invitation in them getting involved in a new social action project:

> When [the vicar] arrived, he saw in me someone who is quite open, rather vocal and he thought it would work. He asked me to be involved and I said yes, it's exactly what I like doing. I like to be proactive and help with doing what Jesus said, which is be wherever people need you. It seemed to me that's what this project was about.

Being asked to take part can also be a marker of someone's belonging and recognition as part of the church community, especially if the role they have been invited to take on fits with their gifts as an individual. Not only is this a practical expression of their value within the community, but it is also a significant point for many people's discipleship journey.

There are parallels here with the way Jesus asked his disciples to follow him. The original journey of discipleship began with a simple invitation, not with the expectation of fully formed theology or profession of belief or even a full understanding of who Jesus was. They were disciples because they had begun following and spending time with Jesus, quite literally without knowing the end of the story. As one interviewee put it, it is possible to be growing in discipleship and "learning the traits of the kingdom" through practical actions "before knowing in full that you are following the king of the kingdom". Social action can provide the context for this invitation.

One individual who had recently taken on a position of lay leadership said:

> That's another thing [this church] does, they put you in areas that might interest you and ask if you'd like to do things. They'll help you. You just feel needed, you feel welcome and you feel worthwhile coming. But also personally it helps.

The story of the feeding of the 5,000 connects invitation, participation and the valorisation of individual gifts, and might thus be a model for social action and discipleship in the church today. When Jesus asks his disciples to feed the five thousand, it is the invitation they then extend to the little boy to share his lunch that facilitates the miracle of feeding. Similarly, we might suggest that the church grows when those who are already part of it invite others to join in the act of loving their community. In the biblical account of this miracle, there is also an implication that the disciples themselves did not have

Fifty-seven-year-old T (Teresa) is unemployed. She struggled to put food on the table, and often went hungry. She began volunteering at the foodbank in August, and shops at the social supermarket. Through this, she has come to faith.

"A while ago, I stopped eating. I didn't have that much food in my house. I'm not going to go asking people for food. Then, I saw about the food bank. I'm unemployed and I asked if I could volunteer. I came in August and I have never left.

"I love the comfort I get here. I can talk to them and they're not judging me. It's nice helping other people. It occupies my time. When I come here, I feel fulfilled. If I weren't here, I'd be making myself sleep, especially on miserable days like today. It's saved me, personally.

"I shop at the social supermarket. There's tinned stuff, fresh vegetables and lots and lots of bread and eggs and often toiletries. You can make a few decent meals out of what you can get for £3.

"It means I won't go hungry. I have enough to last. I have shopped this week and so I can give a can of corn to my neighbour. That's a lovely feeling. It makes me feel happy. I feel valued and appreciated. I'm lucky, very lucky. I've got more than a lot of people.

"I was brought up as a Catholic, but I didn't go to church from where I was 13. I knew there was a God, but I didn't know who he was. Here, I know what I believe. I've got more than I bargained for. Now, I would describe myself as contented. I haven't got no money, or a tablet, or a phone. I'm in debt, but do you know what, I'm contented. The Big J [Jesus] has plans for me."

enough to feed the crowd. Inviting others to join them was a necessity, just as inviting others to join us in social action is necessary to fulfil the purpose of the church.

Discipleship is deepened when people find in social action a new way of expressing their gifts and their faith, even when they have been part of the church for a long time.

In one case study parish, the church secured funding to offer packed lunches to the families attending the breakfast club during the school holidays. Recognising that the existing holiday club volunteers were already stretched, the vicar invited the Mothers' Union to help with making the sandwiches. This was acknowledged as a way they might be able to contribute to the holiday club, drawing on their prior experience of preparing buffets for church events. Most of them were elderly and had previously felt that this limited their capacity to get involved.

Initially, some of them expressed resentment about the fact that the families were given two meals for free and they were described as reluctant to interact with the holiday club guests. Over time, however, instead of sitting in the side room making sandwiches and putting bags of fruit together, they began to leave the door open so they could see the families. Some of the women slowly started to go out and meet the families, sharing hot drinks and conversation with them. By the end of the first summer, they asked if they could be involved again at the October half-term holiday club.

There was just this sense that for years, they'd been told they couldn't do anything because they were too old, but now they could.

Together with the vicar, they developed a way of creatively transforming their sandwich making into an act of worship, rendering it almost liturgical in nature. The vicar printed sheets of paper with the words of Hebrews 13:2 – "Do not forget to show hospitality to strangers, for by doing so some people have shown hospitality to angels without knowing it." – along with a short blessing that they could say together as they prepared the packed lunches.

> *The Mothers' Union now feels that they've got a role in one of our biggest ministries, which is breakfast club. We've just turned sandwich making into an act of worship with prayer. It's two hours a week, but it's become something important.*

The act of service of preparing lunches has here become a key act of worship taking people deeper in their long-held faith and strengthening their sense of belonging to a church community that many of them have been part of for decades. This is an easily replicable way of making a simple, practical contribution to the social action of the church into a fundamentally spiritual act, gently integrating worship with service of the community.

This 'liturgy of sandwich making' is an example of how church social action can avoid the risk of becoming "bland volunteerism", against which we might caution.[19] Integrating simple acts of prayer and worship within social action can negate this.

We heard from several volunteers who do not profess a faith themselves but who acknowledge the value of the volunteer team praying together at the start of a session, particularly in the context of food banks. They articulate this not just as a spiritual act for those who shared the Christian faith, but also as an expression of care for each other as a team.

One individual noted, for example, how inspiring they found
it when people remembered others' prayer requests from a
previous week and asked how the situation has changed, seeing
this as a sign of genuine compassion. In the age of austerity, an
increasing number of food bank volunteers have no religious
faith, and are seemingly motivated by political ideology rather
than theology,[20] but this should not be seen as reason for the
church to shy away from demonstrating faith amongst its
volunteers.

There is a diverse range of reasons why people volunteer
in church-based social action, not all explicitly theological, and
these often evolve in the process. Participation in social action
has the capacity to change the volunteer profoundly. We heard
numerous testimonies of people whose attitudes to others
had shifted towards compassion, even where they approached
social action with paternalistic or arrogant attitudes. For some,
participation in social action is their first personal encounter
with the reality that poverty and deprivation exist in their
community.

> Volunteering at food bank has opened up a whole new world
> which I knew existed but never met.

For civil society, the benefits of volunteering for wellbeing
are well recognised. Participation can combat isolation,
engender a sense of belonging to a community and is also
beneficial to mental health. The act of being involved in
something can be as much a catalyst for transformation as
the initiative itself.[21] Within the church, we observe that this
extends to spiritual wellbeing and discipleship. The second of
the two greatest commandment given by Jesus in the gospels
– to love your neighbour as yourself – was cited numerous
times by research participants as a reason for the church to do

social action, as an expression of love towards its neighbours. In this phrase, the 'as' is often seen as a quantifier: we are being asked to love our neighbours 'as much' as we love ourselves. However, it might also be seen as an expression of the simultaneity of the two actions – the process of learning to love yourself and to love God as you engage in loving others. Participation in social action in whatever form can be transformative for individual wellbeing and discipleship, thus growing the health and strength of the church collectively.

Our capacity to demonstrate love to those around us is important not only for our own discipleship, but also for how others are drawn to faith and thus how the church grows.

The sociologist of religion Peter Berger coined the concept of plausibility structures, the sociocultural conditions of belief systems that render the beliefs plausible.[22] The existence and strength of these structures are what makes it more or less likely that someone who doesn't hold a particular belief system might be convinced of its value and validity. They also help us filter out ideas that are unreasonable or unbelievable within a particular worldview.

Whilst Berger's original concept focused on these structures primarily as something cognitive or intellectual, there is perhaps a practical dimension as well. We might consider the social action of the church as forming part of the plausibility structures of Christianity in as much as it reflects the goodness of the Christian God as expressed in the gospel. If people recognise the church, both locally and nationally, as a place where good things happen, then it increases the plausibility that the belief systems behind it are also good.

The 'goodness' of the church as an institution is seen in its local incarnation. Community outreach renders plausible the goodness of the God who inspires it and a faith that compels individuals to serve others is more plausible than one that doesn't. The opposite is also painfully true; a church that malfunctions serves as an implausibility structure or a hindrance to the gospel, as evidenced by the effects of various safeguarding scandals within the church. As Lesslie Newbigin wrote, "the only possible hermeneutic of the gospel is a congregation which believes it".[23]

In other words, people may be attracted to the church as a community before they are attracted to or convinced by the Christian message. Throughout the research, we have heard stories of people coming to church initially because they were interested in volunteering, then discovering and joining the community of faith as a result: people both give and receive within the church community, but the giving can sometimes come first. In several case studies, participants spoke about how their journey of faith had begun with seeing the social action of the church. In terms of Grace Davie's paradigm of believing and belonging, we might suggest these people sought to belong to something and put that into practice through social action prior to believing fully.[24]

One case study parish is involved in supporting refugees and asylum seekers both within and beyond their community through coordinating aid trips to Calais. In doing so, the church has become well known locally as a collection point and attracted local media attention for its work. People who first heard about the church through this have joined the congregation and come to faith:

> I saw a Facebook post about this church. It was about the collection for the refugee aid trips. I just thought, "This is a

church that's actually living out the gospel. I have to go and see what's happening". So we did and we never left.

This individual had limited prior experience of the Christian faith, but had not been part of a worshipping community for over twenty years. Several other people who had recently joined this church from little or no church background spoke about how they had been drawn to the church –to this church in particular – because of hearing about the good work it was doing.

In this community and elsewhere, many individuals without any experience of church or Christianity still understood the centrality of loving our neighbours to the Christian faith and were interested by a community they perceived as putting that into practice. While these individuals are clearly intrigued by the idea of faith to a degree, they are not necessarily people who would have responded to an invitation to an evangelistic event or course as their first interaction with the church. Instead, they are inherently attracted by the goodness of the church's practical faith in the community and by the power of the invitation to join in. This speaks to the gift-oriented aspect of humanity, modelling the church as a community that needs help and support itself, rather than being self-sufficient.

One individual described their congregation thus:

Being involved in the community, it's almost as if that's how people get involved in sharing what takes place, it's just a great form of mission. You get involved with things, matters of justice and helping build community, and there's just something inherently good about it that attracts people.

David grew up on one of Hoxton's council estates. His father was a major drug dealer there. David also had a drug addiction (from which he is clean), and has been to prison four times. He became a Christian through an Alpha course and is now an outreach worker for St John's Church.

"Because of my addiction I had done a lot of things that I wasn't proud of. My Dad was known as the local drug dealer. Growing up, I felt a lot of shame around that. So, I want to re-write the history. I'm more than a child of a drug addict. This is my way of righting the wrongs of my past. It's about helping other kids. I don't want them to go down the path that I took.

"I regret the things that I have done. What I'm doing today, I can say to God, "Look, you know you heard me and from that moment, I turned my life around". I want a different future for the young people. That's why I'm involved in the church.

"We are looking to set up a mentoring scheme. We want to match people up with mentors from 15-18 years old and give them opportunities that they might not get.

"I remember in rehab they said that a grateful addict will never use again. I wake up with peace of mind and I live on the same estate that I always did. I'm grateful that I don't have to use. I thank God. It's that simple.

"I get paid for the job at St John's, but I don't need the money. I've lived here all my life, and I'm not going anywhere. I'm just little old me, happy in my flat with my wife and my dog and this church is the beacon of hope for us. This is where we belong. That's why we are involved. It's not just listening to the sermon. I feel we need to be involved."

When the church is engaged in social action, it looks most like what people outside it expect it to be and this integrity is attractive to them. The social action tradition is often the element of church life that those who do not belong to recognise when the liturgical or theological dimensions are either harder to comprehend or simply less attractive to them.

In John 13:35 (NIV), Jesus makes the link between social action and discipleship clear when he says that, "by this everyone will know that you are my disciples, if you love one another." Growth and discipleship because of social action stems as much from the church's reputation for action as it does from the action itself. The church grows when it is known for the good that it does and provides opportunities for others to join in with it and therefore to encounter the God behind it all.

Questions to consider

— What opportunities are there for people in the community to get (more) involved in your church's social action?

— Does your church regularly invite people to join in social action, both those inside and outside the congregation?

— How might you develop the practice of invitation around your social action?

1   Helen Cameron, Deborah Bhatti, Catherine Duce, James Sweeney and Clare
    Watkins, *Talking About God in Practice:* Theological Action Research and
    Practical Theology (London: SCM Press, 2010), p. 54, italics the authors'.

2   Paul Bickley, *People, Place and Purpose: Churches and Neighbourhood Resilience in
    the North East* (London: Theos, 2018).

3   Institute for Government, *Local Government Funding in England,* (2020)
    available online at: www.instituteforgovernment.org.uk/explainers/
    local-government-funding-england

4   Based on data from 2018 provided by Church of England Research and
    Statistics.

5   Church of England Research and Statistics, *Statistics for Mission...*

6   Hattie Williams, 'Chelmsford diocese set to cut 60 stipendiary posts
    in the next 18 months', *Church Times,* 9 June 2020, available online
    at: www.churchtimes.co.uk/articles/2020/12-june/news/uk/
    chelmsford-diocese-set-to-cut-60-stipendiary-posts-in-the-next-18-months.

7   Church Growth Research Programme, *From Anecdote to Evidence...*

8   Rick Richardson, *You Found Me: New Research on How Unchurched Nones,
    Millennials, and Irreligious Are Surprisingly Open to Christian Faith* (Illinois: IVP
    Books, 2019).

9   Chris Allen, 'Food Poverty and Christianity in Britain: A Theological Re-
    Assessment' *Political Theology,* 17:4, (2016), pp. 361-377.

10 Charles Roding Pemberton, *Bread of Life...* p. 84.

11 Helen Cameron, Deborah Bhatti, Catherine Duce, James Sweeney and Clare
    Watkins, *Talking About God...* p. 54.

12 Church Urban Fund, *Church in Action 2017...*

13 Norman Wirzba, *Food and Faith: A Theology of Eating* (Cambridge: Cambridge
    University Press, 2011), p. 136

14 Sara Miles, *Take This Bread: A Radical Conversion* (New York: Ballantine Books,
    2008).

15 Church Army Research Unit, *Playfully Serious: How Messy Churches Create New
    Space For Faith* (2019), available online at churcharmy.org/Publisher/File.
    aspx?ID=225713

16 Martin Charlesworth and Natalie Williams, *A Church for the Poor* (Colorado
    Springs: David C Cook, 2017).

17 Luke 5:31, New International Version.

18 Church Growth Research Programme, *From Anecdote to Evidence...*

19 Samuel Wells with Russell Rook and David Barclay, *For Good: The Church*...p. 49.

20 Andrew Williams et al., 'Contested space...' p. 2301.

21 David Boyle, *The Grammar of Change: Big Local neighbourhoods in action* (Local Trust, 2017), available online at: localtrust.org.uk/insights/essays/the-grammar-of-change-an-essay-by-david-boyle/

22 Peter Berger, *The Sacred Canopy: Elements of a Sociological Theory of Religion* (New York: Doubleday, 1969).

23 Lesslie Newbigin, *The Gospel in a Pluralistic Society* (Grand Rapids, Michigan: Eerdmans Publishing Company, 1989).

24 Grace Davie, *Religion in Britain Since 1945: Believing Without Belonging* (Chichester: John Wiley & Sons, 1994).

4

What helps churches
grow? Statistical insights

Having considered the characteristics of growing and flourishing churches according to our qualitative research, we now turn to the quantitative element of the research, exploring the insights that new and existing data can offer into church growth and its relationship with social action and discipleship. This chapter begins with analysis of the 2018 **Statistics for Mission** data[1], followed by analysis and explanation of survey data from our research in Liverpool diocese.

a. Characteristics of church growth

According to the literature, many of the factors that contribute to church growth are characteristics of the congregation, its culture and its leadership, rather than demographic factors about the parish itself. Nevertheless, it is worth examining from the existing quantitative data whether there are any shared demographic characteristics of growing or declining churches.

In this section, we therefore describe characteristics about the churches that are either growing or declining based on their usual Sunday attendance. Unless otherwise stated, analysis is based on the 2018 *Statistics for Mission* data provided by the Church of England's Research and Statistics team.

For the purposes of this analysis, classifications of congregation size are calculated in terms of terciles of attendance. In other words, a third of Anglican churchgoers attend small churches, a third medium and a third large respectively. By this measure, small churches are those with a usual Sunday attendance of 0-53, medium churches 54-116 and large churches have a usual Sunday attendance of 117+. Further explanation is included in Appendix 2.

— Firstly, **urban parishes are more likely to be changing (i.e. growing or declining) than rural ones, but also more likely to be shrinking.**

It appears that the urban or rural nature of a parish has a stronger correlation to the size of the congregation than with its propensity for growth.

Urban congregations are more likely than rural ones to be classed as large. 3% of rural parishes have large congregations according to usual Sunday attendance, compared with 17% of urban parishes. Conversely, the vast majority (86%) of rural parishes are small, compared with fewer than half (44%) of urban parishes. A similar pattern is also observed with respect to average weekly attendance. Some of this may be attributed to contextual factors like differing parish populations and the higher prevalence of team ministry structures in rural areas.

In terms of growth trends, urban congregations are more likely to be *changing*, with 57% demonstrating a conclusive trend for either growth or decline, compared to 46% of rural parishes. However, with this, they are also more likely to be *declining* than rural parishes: 49% of urban parishes are seen to be conclusively declining, as opposed to 35% of rural parishes. By contrast, rural parishes (11%) are marginally more likely to be growing than their urban counterparts (8%).

— Secondly, **how deprived a parish is does not significantly affect growth (though the extremes fare badly).**

Parishes in more deprived areas are no less likely to be growing than those in less deprived communities. When parishes are ranked from most to least deprived according to the Index of Multiple Deprivation, there is a near-equal distribution of growing churches across the scale.

However, there is a greater proportion of declining congregations among both the most deprived quintile and least deprived quintile than in the middle three quintiles. In other words, the most deprived and least deprived parishes in the country are equally likely to be declining, but both are more likely to be declining than the parishes in between.

— Thirdly, **parishes with smaller populations are more likely to be growing.**

There is a possible connection between the size of the parish population and the growth or decline of the local church. On average, growing churches have a smaller parish population than those that are declining. The mean parish population among growing churches is 3,667, compared to 5,122 for declining churches and 4,282 across all categories. For context, the largest parish population nationally is 75,650 and the smallest is 14. Understood through the lens of the Anglican parish model, which means that clergy have the cure of souls of all parishioners, this might be interpreted as suggesting that is easier to grow a church when the clergy resource is less stretched. However, some of the smallest parishes by population are in multi-parish benefices where clergy are stretched across multiple parishes.

Rural parishes that are growing have smaller parish populations on average than declining rural parishes and also than the whole subset of rural parishes.

There are limits to this; exceptionally small parish populations (e.g. rural parishes with <50 residents) are not proportionally more likely to grow than parishes with slightly larger populations. The smallest quintile of parishes by population is overwhelmingly rural and over 99% of these also have small congregations.

— Calculating church attendance as a proportion of parish population offers some illustration of the dynamic of a parish, but there are some contextual factors at play.

Nationally, the average weekly attendance represents 1.5% of the population and the usual Sunday attendance 1.2%. The worshipping community is close to 2% of the population.

Among growing churches, the usual Sunday attendance represents on average 9.1% of the size of the parish population and the worshipping community 11%. Among declining churches, these figures are 2.3% and 4.2% respectively. Growing churches of all sizes have a higher attendance as a proportion of their parish population size than those that are declining or inconclusive.

Those with the largest attendance as a percentage of the parish population are almost all city centre parishes with growing, gathered congregations and small resident populations. Cathedrals, for example, fit this profile. At the upper extreme, one city centre parish's attendance figures represent over 2000% of its parish population, but the population is only 44.

(The data do not measure the proportion of the congregation who are resident in the parish; it is possible to have an attendance numerically equivalent to the entire parish population without any of the congregation living in the parish.)

— It is important to recognise that **attendance and participation data, and the growth trends they display, must be seen in the local context.**[2]

Many of the findings outlined above are likely attributable to contextual factors and changes in the parish population. From the available data, it is not possible to interrogate fully if and where population change in a parish may have influenced church growth or decline. If the population of a geographical parish grows significantly due to a new housing development or similar, we might observe a different dynamic of growth compared to a congregation that grows actively in the context of a static population. Conversely, if a parish population declines – for example due to the demolition or regeneration of an area of housing – then the congregation may shrink and the nature of ministry in the parish will likely evolve. Both these situations require contextualisation to disentangle the different factors and dynamics of growth and decline.

Population changes may also mean that growth where it occurs is not always apparent in the ten-year statistical trends. For example, in a parish where the population is constantly changing but church attendance has remained stable, the congregation has effectively grown and declined in equal measure, but will show up as inconclusive and thus mask the growth that has occurred. We observe this to be the case in a number of the qualitative case study parishes, where a number of the congregation have left or passed away but the congregation has remained stable due to a similar number of newcomers. In other circumstances, this would constitute growth.

As this analysis has shown, there are various descriptive factors of parishes and their context that can and do influence church growth. However, none of them are enough to ensure growth, or to explain growth in any given parish in isolation. Neither are these necessarily characteristics that congregations can intentionally develop or cultivate. It is therefore important to consider also where social action and discipleship fit in to the narrative of growing churches.

b. Quantitative survey results

As previously explained, the planned quantitative survey was hindered by the COVID-19 pandemic. In the end, we were able to obtain 120 responses from 22 parishes in three deaneries in the diocese of Liverpool. The profile of these parishes is largely suburban, with moderate levels of deprivation and relative little demographic diversity. We do not therefore claim that the analysis given here is nationally representative, but it still offers some insights of wider relevance. Unlike the qualitative research, due to the timing of the survey, it is also able to hint at how the church's role and capacity for social action is being changed by the pandemic.

Due to the sample size, we were not able to analyse the data fully in relation to church growth trends or congregation size. For example, only six respondents (5%) were from growing churches – in this case, one single church – and while this is broadly representative of the deaneries involved, it is too small a sample to draw any significant conclusions and still maintain anonymity.

So too, by coincidence rather than design, the participants were split equally into those who were under 65 years old and those who gave their age as 65 or over. For this reason, we chose to run analysis of these two groups to see if and whether they diverged. Where this was the case, we note that. In particular, with reference to the questions on COVID-19 and its effects on volunteering, it was felt this was a relevant avenue to investigate due to the greater likelihood of those over 65 being required to shield and therefore unable to participate as actively as before.

How does social action help make connections in your community?

The majority of respondents (57%) agreed that they first met people who worshipped at that particular church through church-based community activities. This emphasises the potential importance of social action in growing the relational networks of the church and also of individual congregation members. While a majority also said that they had made friends through volunteering in church-based community action, over 65s were more likely to agree strongly with this statement; 43% of over 65s strongly agreed, compared to 26% of under 65s.

A majority (54%) of respondents were unsure whether people who first came into contact with their church through community action have become Christians, although only 5% actually disagreed with this statement and 0% strongly disagreed. As we go on to explore in the recommendations, this raises questions about whether churches and their leaders are effectively encouraging their congregations to make the connection between social action, discipleship and growth.

What led you to get involved in social action?

Participants were asked to consider the activities they were frequently involved in before the pandemic and select from a list of twelve up to three reasons which had led them to get involved.

Over 65s were almost twice as likely to say that they had benefitted personally from the church's social action and wanted to give back. 17% gave this as a motivating factor for their involvement while only 9% of under 65s did.

Under 65s were more likely to say that they had become aware that there are people in need of help in the community and they wanted to help to make a difference. 26% of under 65s selected this option, making it the third most popular answer. By contrast, it was the third least popular answer among over 65s, selected by 14%.

Under 65s were more likely to say that feeling called by God to be involved had been important, with 38% saying this compared to 27% of over 65s.

I feel that helping my community has...

Participants were asked to select from a list of ten the three statements they most strongly agreed with in terms of the effect that helping their community had had on them personally.

The most popular answer in all age groups was 'helped me build friendships with people in the community that I would not have met otherwise', with 61% of people selecting this. Again, this reinforces the findings of the qualitative research that social action is instrumental in bringing congregations into relationship with those they might not otherwise encounter, which we argue is critical for church growth and discipleship through social action.

Over 65s were significantly more likely than under 65s to feel that helping their community had made them more generous with their money; 18% of over 65s chose this as one of their three statements compared to 4% of under 65s.

Over 65s were slightly more likely to say helping had increased their commitment to their faith, with 26% selecting this compared to 20% of under 65s. Conversely, under 65s were more likely (20% v 14%) to say it had raised questions which are challenging to faith. The statements relating directly to faith were broadly speaking less popular or less selected than the ones pertaining to practical implications and relationships, which leads us to suggest that the connection between social action and discipleship is not always explicit and could be highlighted more.

Encouragingly, only 4% of under 65s and 0% of over 65s reported that helping their community had left them drained or discouraged.

COVID-19 pandemic and resulting changes

Participants were asked how their church's offer of support to the community has changed since the pandemic, how their own involvement has changed and what they feel the result of this might be for the church and community post-pandemic. Again, it should be highlighted that is not a nationally representative sample but the age brackets of participants offer helpful indications.

Overall, 43% of respondents felt their church was doing more than before. 27% said it was doing about the same as before. 23% felt their church was doing less than before. 7% did not know. On a personal level, 21% of respondents said they were more involved than before. A third said they were doing about the same as before. 47% of respondents said they were doing less than before.

Almost twice as many people felt their church was doing more than before as felt they personally were doing more. The reverse is also true; over twice as many people (47%) said they personally were less involved than before than felt that their church as a whole was doing less (23%).

Under 65s (27%) were more likely than over 65s (18%) to say their personal involvement has increased since the onset of the pandemic. The reverse is also true; 49% of over 65s say they are doing less, compared to 38% of under 65s. This bears out the hypothesis that involvement has been affected by predominantly older people being required to shield and therefore unable to be physically involved. A number of people commented that they are still involved in supporting through prayer despite not being able to contribute practically to the same extent as before.

Thinking ahead to when the current crisis ends, 33% said they thought their church would be more engaged with the community. 59% said they thought their church would be more aware of the community's needs and 36% felt their church would be more able to offer support. 17% felt the church's engagement with its community would be unchanged and 13% thought their church would be less able to offer support to the community than before the crisis.

Not all of those who felt their church would be more aware of the community's needs felt they would also be more able to offer support or more engaged with the community, suggesting respondents are mindful of limitations on their capacity. Again, this is reflected in the written responses, many of which commented on the lack of capacity in the congregation.

1 This section draws on the 2018 release of *Statistics for Mission* data, which was the most recent available at the time the analysis was carried out. The 2019 data has subsequently been released.

2 Church of England Research and Statistics, *Statistics for Mission* 2018 (London: Church of England Research and Statistics, 2019), available online at: www.churchofengland.org/sites/default/files/2019-10/2018StatisticsForMission_0.pdf

5
Conclusion and recommendations

Church growth is not the primary goal of social action; the gospels suggest that Jesus rejected the instrumental generosity of his day:

> *When you give a luncheon or dinner, do not invite your friends, your brothers or sisters, your relatives, or your rich neighbours; if you do, they may invite you back and so you will be repaid. But when you give a banquet, invite the poor, the crippled, the lame, the blind, and you will be blessed. (Luke 14:12b-13, NIV)*

Whilst some Christian thinkers might articulate an instrumental vision of social action – i.e., one where it is carried out explicitly in order to grow the church or evangelise people – this was not the case for the churches we visited in this research. None of them expressed having got involved in social action because they expected "repayment" in the form of conversions or higher attendance.

However, social action does affect churches beneficially and, as we have seen, can lead to the growth of the congregation corporately and individually. In a secularising society where people no longer feel an inherent sense of warmth towards the church, it helps people cross barriers of religious identity and non-identity. Whether with people who approach the church for help, or people who want to work with others to provide help, through social action churches come into relationship with people who do not identify with church or Christianity, and may even have sought it out for practical rather than purely spiritual motivations.

Prior to the pandemic, the Church of England already found itself at a kind of tipping point. In light of the events of 2020, it is clearer still that what exists in the future will not be the same as what has existed in the past. The church's social role is ever more important and the church should embrace it even more than it already has, and acknowledge that this is now a key pillar of its establishment in any sense other than the barest constitutional form.

With this in mind, we offer the following recommendations.

a. For the national church institutions
— Firstly, we suggest that a **national Church of England volunteering service should be** established to build relationships and connect people of goodwill to local projects.

The response to calls for community and volunteering assistance during the pandemic evidenced that our collective desire to contribute to the common good and the wellbeing of our neighbours is a huge and untapped force the church might be well-placed to mobilise. Nearly a million individuals signed up to be NHS volunteer responders supporting people in the community but few were ultimately called upon.[1] Many of these were individuals on furlough or recently unemployed, who would not usually be able to contribute during working hours, but who showed a willingness to give their time to help others. Research found that the growth of mutual aid groups was largely driven by those on furlough who were not previously involved in volunteering.[2]

The pandemic led to a large group of people beyond the 'usual suspects' becoming interested and active in community social action, but the question remains, how can it be mobilised? National government is too distant from communities, and local government has been pared back to bare essentials, and seemingly lacks the capacity or creativity to open up these reserves of social capital.

Parish churches could be an excellent vehicle to engage people of all faiths and none in looking to the needs of their neighbours. As we have said, different congregations engage with different levels of sophistication, but even the smallest and weakest congregations have the power to befriend, tackling issues around loneliness and isolation. A Church of England volunteering service could see people register to help and be immediately directed to opportunities in their locality. Churches are already used to vetting, training and supporting people in volunteering roles. Meanwhile churches that could evidencing appropriate safeguarding and governance standards, register to benefit from a new source of volunteers. In many ways, this could simply formalise what we already see happening organically in communities across England.

— Secondly, we recommend that **an additional metric of church size could be introduced, broader still than the Worshipping Community measure.**

There is a demonstrable connection between social action, discipleship and the growth of the church, where that social action is aided by sustained presence, an awareness of life's complexity, a culture of generosity and hospitality and the invitation to participate. However, we also conclude that the ways in which this growth occurs are not always captured by current quantitative metrics – above all, the prioritisation of Sunday attendance as a measure of meaningful growth – and there is therefore a risk that the church does not recognise it. Where the church is growing through social action and in complex situations, it often does so at the fringes and in ways that may not be counted numerically in average attendances.

There are reasons to question whether regular Sunday attendance remains the most meaningful metric of congregation life in a modern age. This, like so much else, has been re-examined during the COVID-19 pandemic and lockdown period. In order to mitigate the economic impact of the pandemic, there have been attempts to relax the Sunday trading laws further, and it would be naïve to think that Sunday maintains the same importance in society as it once did. There is a need for a balance between reiterating the importance of the Sabbath in the Christian tradition, no matter how counter-cultural it is, and accepting the changing mores of society. Whilst the pandemic may have rendered church services physically impossible, the proliferation of online services has made worship more accessible in some senses.

Current metrics privilege regular attendance at services over the depth of discipleship that may occur at the fringe, and thus, even prior to the pandemic, have not been capturing the full growth and depth of the church. It was already observed that many church leaders "now speak of an 'active fringe' rather than a 'committed core'," which perhaps better reflects societal patterns.[3]

In a number of case studies, clergy quoted this number as an indication of the church's footprint in the local community and in most cases it was significantly larger than the attendance. Footfall in the church building or social action project does not automatically render someone part of the church's worshipping community, but it indicates that they might one day be. We are mindful that in current circumstances, church buildings do not represent the hubs of community action to the same extent they typically do and do not wish to reduce the church to what happens in the building. However, some consideration of the number of people who come into the building each week for social action activities and if/how that differs from those who worship there is still valuable.

It is important that this is not interpreted as an attempt to simply 'spin' or tell a better story about the growth of the Church of England than the data currently suggest. It would not refute the accepted reality of a church whose attendance and affiliation is in continual decline, and changing the way growth and health is measured would not itself lead to growth. However, it would provide a richer picture of where and how growth is – and isn't – occurring. It might also begin to highlight the enduring importance and convening power of the Church of England to local communities in a way that isn't fully expressed by attendance or affiliation.

If the church is growing in dispersal as well as gathering, it affects the community around it, leading to a growth in social action and discipleship as well. It would be too reductive to suggest that measuring growth in social action – e.g. an increase in volunteer hours – could be a proxy for church growth, but there is a need for a more expansive understanding of what church growth is.

Prompted by the pandemic, there is an acknowledgement that this year in particular, the normal metrics are insufficient in conveying the growth and presence of the church. For example, there has been no such thing as a 'usual Sunday' this year and such, the Church of England's Research and Statistics team do not intend to collect data on the usual Sunday attendance. Instead, there will be data collected on the other types of church offering, whether face to face, online or a hybrid variety of 'church at home'. Churches will be asked about how many people they think they have engaged and given a chance to recount the stories, rather than only to count the figures. There is a clear recognition that churches should be enabled to report what they have done this year that they are proud of, in a way that can be celebrated, whether that is qualitatively or quantitatively.

This approach is to be welcomed and is not dissimilar from the sort of approach this report might have recommended regardless of the pandemic. Although driven by the extraordinary circumstances of 2020, it is true in other years too that the stories that are most celebrated in parishes – the individual who no longer runs away from the police, or the toddler group mum who has begun asking questions about faith – are not always captured in statistical metrics. Numerical growth and attendance remains a valid aspect of church life and we do not suggest it should be disregarded. Rather we recommend that it should be considered together with other accounts of growth and that this should continue in the years after the COVID-19 pandemic.

— Further to this, we also recommend that **any measurement of church growth should be contextual, whether it measures attendance, engagement or encounter.**

Current measures of church growth rely on congregational statistics and do not integrate parish population data. They do not thus factor in the effect of the changing population of a parish on the congregational trend. We suggest that doing so would deepen our understanding of how context affects growth in areas of high population churn, something that wasn't possible in our analysis.

For national and local church leaders, this would also allow them to understand growth and decline in context, in a similar way to how the education system assesses a school's exam results in the context of its catchment area. For example, the leadership of a primary school in a deprived neighbourhood might consider a variety of indicators when assessing its performance, including the progress made by pupils, their backgrounds and the context.

— In order for the church to grow in numbers and depth through social action, **funding and resourcing structures also need to accommodate this**.

There were concerns expressed by participants that the Strategic Development Fund has introduced into the working of the church some of the same constraints as statutory funding, namely short-term finance and a reliance on measuring impact. Much of this is pragmatically driven; the church does need to ensure its long-term financial strength as well as the sustainability of mission in a place, and the sums of money involved in SDF bids are large enough to require accountability. However, overly mechanistic approaches to growth risk inadvertently losing the spirit of what the church is and does.

This might also mean resourcing a commitment to presence in places where this is hard. The church's longevity and willingness to last the course should be evidenced in its financial commitment to parishes as well as the cultural and emotional resilience needed.

b. For church leaders and congregations

The characteristics outlined in chapter 3 emphasise the importance of congregational culture and identity in connecting social action with church growth and discipleship. This is instructive for clergy and church leaders in considering

how to develop this culture in their congregation, not only
initiate new social action projects.

— The local church should **think more strategically about
the potential of its social action and volunteering to lead to
growth.**

Churches are sometimes surprised when those outside the
congregation want to volunteer with them, but as our research
finds, participation in social action is a key way in which
people first come into relationship with the church. A majority
of our survey respondents said that they first met people who
worshipped at that particular church through church-based
community activities.

Above, we have recommended a new Church of England
volunteering service, making the most of the groundswell
of willing volunteers after the pandemic. Whether that
happens or not, churches should cultivate a greater openness
to this possibility and the growth to which it may lead, by
intentionally inviting people to participate in social action,
not only to attend. Churches can often focus on invitation in
terms of social events or discipleship courses such as Alpha but
should equally see their social action projects as primary sites
of invitation and be expectant of the relationships that can
grow through it.

— Churches should **explicitly include the relationship
between social action and discipleship in their preaching
and teaching,** whether through Sunday sermons, teaching
series, small group studies or otherwise.

This relationship is evident from the data and from our
observations of parishes of all shapes and sizes, but this is
not always recognised by churchgoers. Our survey found that

54% of respondents were unsure whether people who first came into contact with their church through social action had become Christians. Almost a third of respondents (31%) said they find it difficult to invite friends and neighbours to church-based community activities. Given that the majority of respondents (86%) were involved in at least one form of social action in their community, this uncertainty cannot be attributed to a lack of familiarity with social action.

This suggests that while congregations are often good at providing social action and equally good at running discipleship programmes, joining the dots between the two is not always instinctive for volunteers. There is a clear gap between people doing social action, them knowing how to link it explicitly to their faith and then sharing their faith.

Church Urban Fund research in 2012 highlighted "an apparent lack of awareness of poverty among the laity", with data showing that 37% of regular churchgoers thought there was "quite a lot" of child poverty in Britain, compared to 78% of clergy.[4] More churchgoers in the study attributed poverty to laziness than to social injustice. Among both churchgoers and the non-religious, 38% felt that poverty was "an inevitable part of modern life", whereas only 12% of clergy agreed with this statement. This emphasises the need for discipleship to be more explicitly connected to social action and vice versa. Part of the process of discipleship, of becoming more like Jesus, might involve a softening of some of the attitudes expressed above and this cannot be disconnected from the practicalities of social action. Involvement in social action is a practical form of discipleship and can profoundly change the individual as well as the community they are seeking to serve.

— We suggest that **more resources might be developed to connect social action and discipleship for use by congregations and church leaders.**

This could include a 'How to Make a Difference' course, open to people of all faiths and none, which would draw people together around the question of why and how they can go about social change. This could be used by congregations in a similar way to Alpha, over a series of weeks, in-person or online. We suggest it could include content on change models such as community organising, asset-based community development, social enterprise and others. It would also discuss theological or philosophical reflections on motivations for involvement in social action, in an open-ended rather than prescriptive manner. This would position the church as a space where it is possible to participate in making a difference without this being seen instrumentally.

These resources could also be adapted to draw out what the relationship looks like in rural parishes, small congregations and other specific contexts, and how to facilitate fruitful integration of action, growth and discipleship in these contexts. It might also include resources to theme these discussions around the church calendar where liturgically appropriate.

— Congregations should be encouraged to **reflect on how the culture of their social action helps or hinders their growth and discipleship.**

As has been noted already, we find that congregational culture is a determining factor in whether growth stems from church social action. It is important for congregations to reflect upon this in their mission action planning. Along with the characteristics of growing churches in this report, we have indicated discussion questions that congregations might like to consider. These could, for example, form part of a PCC meeting, the development of a mission action plan, or a wider conversation with the congregation and community. The questions are designed to stimulate discussion about the particular parish context and the congregational culture; they do not direct the community towards any specific form of action but rather encourage conversation.

This might be developed into an audit of relationships and community involvement, using one of the existing resources for doing so. For example, parish wide listening exercises (e.g. those framed by Partnership for Missional Church or Know Your Church Know Your Neighbourhood) can guide congregations in listening to the needs of the community over several years.

However, it is important that this is balanced with a degree of self-reflection among congregations about their existing activities and the culture around them.

c. Conclusion

Discussing the relative importance of evangelism and social activism in the life of the church, the South American theologian and missiologist René Padilla wrote that it was like trying to assess the relative importance of the right and left wings of an aeroplane.[5] Both aspects should be seen as essential to the life of congregations and, Padilla suggested, there must be an integral relationship between the two if they are to flourish.

Through our qualitative and quantitative exploration, we observe this to be true. More than this, what we often think of as distinct categories of congregational life – social action, discipleship and evangelism – overlap and intertwine in dynamic and contextual ways. Importantly, all are rooted in the quality and quantity of human connection and relationship within and without a church community.

There is no simple or single fix for the challenges faced by the Church of England at a local or national level. Faced with the broader picture of institutional decline, local churches can turn inward and become defensive, trying to protect or retain what exists rather than look for or uncover new possibilities. Where we see churches growing through social action, congregations are on their own journey of learning and relearning what it is to be a Christian community in their context.

As Christian congregations serve their communities, they form new relationships which result in change and growth. Those congregations often grow as people are awakened to and explore their spirituality in the context of Christian community. Social action and discipleship are not the means to the end of church growth; all are important in and of themselves. They belong together, and it is only in pursuing them collectively that the Church of England can continue in its mission as the national church beyond 2020.

1 BBC News, 'Coronavirus: Volunteers 'not being called upon' to help NHS', 24 April 2020, available online at: www.bbc.co.uk/news/uk-52418946

2 Luca Tiratelli and Simon Kaye, *Communities vs. Coronavirus: The Rise of Mutual Aid* (London: New Local, 2020) available at: https://www.newlocal.org.uk/publications/communities-vs-coronavirus-the-rise-of-mutual-aid/

3 Emma Ineson, *Ambition...* p. 61.

4 Church Urban Fund, Bias to the Poor? *Christian Attitudes to Poverty in this Country* (CUF and Church Action on Poverty, 2012).

5 René Padilla, 'The Mission of the Church in Light of the Kingdom of God' in *Transformation: An International Journal of Holistic Mission Studies*, 1:2 (1984), p. 19.

Appendix 1:
Qualitative sampling

This appendix outlines how the qualitative case studies were selected in order to be representative of the Church of England in all its theological, demographic and geographical breadth.

Parishes were chosen based on suggestions from diocesan representatives and preliminary interviewees, which led to a shortlist of over 500 parishes. It was stressed throughout this that the research was interested in parishes that might offer insight into the relationship between church growth, social action and discipleship, which might not be the largest congregations, the ones growing the most or the ones undertaking the most social action in numerical terms.

Geography

At least one parish was chosen from in every diocese in England, with the additional parishes spread evenly across the administrative regions of the country. 49 case studies (74%) were urban and 17 case studies (26%) were rural. Rural parishes more frequently include more than one church and this was reflected in the sample. In a number of places, the case study spanned more than one parish because of the benefice structure, but this was still counted as one case study.

Growth

Because of the focus on church growth within this research, it was decided that a majority of the sample would be drawn from parishes which are considered to be either inconclusive or growing, although the sample would also include a number of parishes which appear to be in decline. By usual Sunday attendance, 19 parishes in the sample (29%) were growing, 15 parishes (23%) were declining and 32 (48%) were inconclusive. Nationally, 10% are growing, 49% declining and 40% inconclusive.

Congregation size

A third of parishes in the sample selected were classed as large, a third as medium and a third as small, according to the definitions explored in appendix 2.

Deprivation

Parishes in the sample ranged from the #1 most deprived parish in the country according to the Index of Multiple Deprivation to a parish ranked in the 1% least deprived.

Theology

Another important variable is the churchmanship or theological outlook of individual parishes, of which there is a diversity within the Church of England. This is not captured in the church's statistical data because it is harder to define as a variable. Through the sampling and research process, efforts were made to ensure the different strands and traditions of the Church of England (e.g. Anglo-Catholic, evangelical, liberal) were well represented. The sample was reassessed regularly and where gaps were identified, these were redressed.

Participants

Participants included clergy, church staff, lay leaders, congregation members, volunteers, guests of church social action and other community stakeholders such as local head teachers. While participants were at no point asked to record their age, gender or ethnicity, consideration was given to ensuring the diversity of interviewees informally. Around 25% of participants were ordained clergy, including at least one in every parish.

Appendix 2: Defining church size

To make sure the sample was representative in terms of church size, we first needed to define size brackets, as there is no standardised definition of what constitutes a small, medium or large congregation in the Church of England. It was initially proposed to calculate these in terms of terciles of parishes i.e. the smallest third of parishes would be classed as small, the next third as medium and the largest third of parishes as large. The size brackets suggested, using 2018 data, were as follows:

	Usual Sunday attendance	Average weekly attendance	Worshipping community
Small	0–17	0–19	0–30
Medium	18–46	20–69	31–85
Large	47–3400	70–3967	86–4155
Median	27	32	42

By these measures, the smallest third of parishes account for only 8% of individual churchgoers by usual Sunday attendance, while the 'large' category would include 71% of individuals. However, this does not necessarily capture the lived reality of church community. For example, we encountered numerous examples of churches whose attendance figures place them firmly in the 'large' category, but who describe themselves as medium or even small.

As William Nye, the secretary-general of General Synod acknowledges, "a lot of people's picture of the norm of the church is a vicar and about 100 people on a Sunday morning."[1] In reality, an attendance of 100 would put a congregation in the largest 20% nationally by both metrics, and the majority of congregations are significantly smaller than that. Whilst the definition of a megachurch suggests a congregation of 2000+, only eight Church of England congregations have a usual Sunday attendance over 1000; these tend to be gathered congregations in city centres.

We addressed this by recalculating the brackets with respect to terciles of people rather than parishes i.e. so that a third of all churchgoers are considered to attend small, medium and large churches respectively. Furthermore, a disproportionate number of small churches by the original measure are rural, which masks that comparatively small churches do exist in urban areas too.

Using 2018 data to calculate these gave the following suggested brackets, shown here along with the proportion of parishes nationally in each bracket:

	Usual Sunday attendance		Average weekly attendance		Worshipping community	
Small	0-53	71%	0-88	73%	0-100	73%
Medium	54-116	21%	89-180	19%	101-227	20%
Large	117-3400	8%	181-3967	8%	228-4155	7%

As we explored previously with respect to numerical growth, there is a discrepancy between the measurement and lived experience of church size. Subjective experience and objective numbers are both valid, although they present slightly divergent pictures of the church here. We chose to use this second model in our sampling process because it fits better with anecdotal understandings of size, borne out subsequently by the qualitative research.

1 Madeleine Davies, 'We are neglecting mid-sized churches,
   Nye admits' Church Times, 22 July 2019, available online at: www.
   churchtimes.co.uk/articles/2019/26-july/news/uk/
   we-are-neglecting-mid-sized-churches-nye-admits

Appendix 3: Quantitative survey sample

This appendix details the sample of respondents to the quantitative survey. The survey received 130 responses from 22 parishes in three selected deaneries in Liverpool diocese.

The demographic profile of respondents was not very diverse by ethnicity or gender; 98% were British. 72% were female and 28% male. With respect to ethnicity in particular, this is much less diverse than the national population, but more closely representative of the parishes involved and therefore their congregations.

In terms of age, almost three quarters (74%) were over 55 years old and nearly half (48%) were over the age of 65. Only 6% were under 35 years old and there were no respondents under the age of 25. The proportion of respondents over the age of 65 is disproportionate to the age profile of the parish populations involved, although BSA data suggests that the typical Anglican congregation is slightly older than the general population on average.

Of a possible 37 parishes in the three deaneries selected, 22 parishes submitted a response. Of these, 7 parishes (32%) had only one respondent. The mean average was 5.6 responses per parish.

In terms of church size, 17% of respondents came from large congregations, 51% from medium congregations and 32% from small congregations.

Appendix 4: Survey questions

1. **Are you involved in the following activities in your church/ community? (Select from: no, never; no, not at the moment; yes, occasionally; yes, regularly; not applicable.)**

   — Helping neighbours with practical or emotional support
   — Raising money for local or national charities
   — Running or helping out at festivals, fetes, or similar community events
   — Helping out at church-run community projects (e.g., foodbank or lunch club)
   — Helping out with projects run by other people or non-church
   — Looking after the local environment or local green spaces (e.g. working in community gardens)
   — Campaigning to change something for the better (e.g. social justice group)
   — Youth activities (e.g. youth club, sports club, Guides, Scouts)
   — Joining residents'/tenants' associations or community action
   — Supporting people with advice, counselling or a listening service
   — Providing debt advice or financial counselling
   — Activities for young families (e.g. toddler groups, Messy Church)
   — Praying for social issues in your local community

2. **Think about the activities that you were most frequently involved in before the COVID-19 pandemic. What things led you to get involved? (Select up to three reasons.)**

   — Being involved in the community is promoted in the preaching and teaching in this church.

- I have benefitted from the church's social action and wanted to give back.
- Study groups in our church often look at the way the Bible encourages social action.
- I became aware that there are people in need of help in the community, and I want to help make a difference.
- Members of our church were personally affected by an issue and the wider church wanted to respond.
- If I didn't get involved, then the activity might not happen.
- People have spiritual and physical needs and I want to help meet both.
- The connections that we make though community action are important for sharing the gospel.
- I want this church to be more recognised as part of the community.
- I was asked to get involved by a friend or contact.
- I felt called by God to be involved.
- I want to use my time, gifts and skills to benefit the community I live in.

3. **I feel that helping my community has... (Select up to three statements you agree with most strongly.)**

    - Increased my sense of compassion for other people.
    - Increased my commitment to my faith.
    - Helped me to understand my faith better.
    - Led me to pray more for my community.
    - Raised questions which are challenging to my faith.
    - Has left me drained or discouraged.
    - Helped me build friendships with people in the community that I would not have met otherwise.

— Helped me speak about my faith with people in my community.
— Made me more generous with my money.
— Helped me empathise with people from different backgrounds to me.

4. **How does social action help make connections in your community? (Select from: strongly agree, agree, disagree, strongly disagree, don't know.)**

— I first met people who worshipped at this church through church-based community activities.
— I have made friends through volunteering in church-based community action.
— This church's community action has brought people from the existing congregation and the wider community together.
— I find it easy to invite friends and neighbours to church services.
— People who first came into contact with our church through community action have become Christians.
— I find it difficult to invite friends and neighbours to church-based community activities.
— My faith is a motivation for me to get involved in other – non-church – community groups.

5. **As far as you are aware, how has your church's offer of support to the community changed since before the pandemic? (Tick one box).**

— About the same as before.
— Doing less than before.
— Doing more than before.
— Don't know.

6. If your church is offering anything new please record it here. (Text box)

7. How has your personal involvement in your church's social action changed since before the pandemic? (Tick one box)

   — About the same as before.
   — Doing less than before.
   — Doing more than before.

8. Thinking ahead to when the current crisis ends, how do you think your church's engagement with its community will have changed compared with before Covid-19? (Tick all that apply)

   — More engaged with the community.
   — More aware of the community's needs.
   — Not changed since before the crisis.
   — More able to offer support to the community.
   — Less able to offer support to the community.

9. Please use this space for any comments you have, which may include the ways in which you've been able to receive or offer support from your church during this situation. (Text box)

Theos – enriching conversations

Theos exists to enrich the conversation about the role of faith in society.

Religion and faith have become key public issues in this century, nationally and globally. As our society grows more religiously diverse, we must grapple with religion as a significant force in public life. All too often, though, opinions in this area are reactionary or ill informed.

We exist to change this

We want to help people move beyond common misconceptions about faith and religion, behind the headlines and beneath the surface. Our rigorous approach gives us the ability to express informed views with confidence and clarity.

As the UK's leading religion and society think tank, we reach millions of people with our ideas. Through our reports, events and media commentary, we influence today's influencers and decision makers. According to *The Economist*, we're "an organisation that demands attention". We believe Christianity can contribute to the common good and that faith, given space in the public square, will help the UK to flourish.

Will you partner with us?

Theos receives no government, corporate or denominational funding. We rely on donations from individuals and organisations to continue our vital work. Please consider signing up as a Theos Friend or Associate or making a one off donation today.

Theos Friends and Students

— Stay up to date with our monthly newsletter

— Receive (free) printed copies of our reports

— Get free tickets to all our events

 £75/ year
for Friends

 £40/ year
for Students

Theos Associates

— Stay up to date with our monthly newsletter

— Receive (free) printed copies of our reports

— Get free tickets to all our events

— Get invites to private events with the Theos team and other Theos Associates

£375/ year

 Sign up on our website:
www.theosthinktank.co.uk/about/support-us